PRAISE FOR
I'M FULL OF IT
AND SO ARE YOU

Daniel Gomer's authenticity brings a fresh voice and perspective to personal development. In *I'm Full of It and So Are You* he declares, «Every individual can change the world,» and reading this book leaves no doubt.

—Courtland Warren - International Speaker

Dan has a keen wit and writes in a style that makes one feel like they are listening to an old friend. *I'm Full of It and So Are You* has not only helped me become more aware of my own negative programming, but has also helped me set an intention to make myself a better person. Read this book, find your purpose, and go make the world a better place. After all, WE'RE ALL FULL OF IT!"

—Chris Driessen, CEO, SLANG Worldwide

Happy,

Stay classy
Stay awesome
Stay Full of IT!

After all, life's too
wild to take it
Seriously.

Here's to your journey!

I'M
FULL
OF IT
AND SO
ARE YOU

LET'S CHANGE THE
WORLD TOGETHER

DANIEL GOMER

I'm Full Of It And So Are You! Let's Change The World Together
Published by Condor Enterprises
Highlands Ranch, Colorado

ISBN: 978-1-7356841-0-9
BISAC Category SELF-HELP / Personal Growth / Success

Cover and Interior design by Victoria Wolf, Wolf Design and Marketing
Editing by Alexandra O'Connell

CONDOR
VENTURES

THIS BOOK IS DEDICATED TO YOU, the reader. Not because I like to pander, although I do thank you for reading, but rather, because, by daring to pick up this book, you display a desire to make yourself better and you are committed to expanding as a human being. This book would not be in your hand if you were not trying to become the best and most powerful version of yourself. It doesn't matter if my thoughts are accurate or complete nonsense, because the power to change the world lies within you and your choice to simply try. Your act of curiosity toward self-discovery is an act of courage, and you should thank yourself for all that you are and all that you can be. All these pages are my contribution toward making the world a better place, and I put these words on paper for you. This book is dedicated to you and your journey. You are powerful beyond belief. Thank you for taking the time to explore. Thank you for taking on the challenge to make yourself better. Thank you for making the world a better place for us all. Here's to your journey, my friend!

CONTENTS

PREFACE

WE ARE ALL WORLD CHANGERS. Like it or not, we change our world every moment of every day, and it doesn't take much effort on our part—when we smile at a stranger, when we argue with a friend, when we hold a grudge, when we show compassion, when we think, and when we speak. We are powerful beings, and it's time we started wielding our tremendous power with care, forethought, and intention.

As many of us get older and as we get caught up in our daily routines, it's easy to forget how much influence we have on the world. The more stuff gets piled on our plate, the less energy we have to explore. We unwittingly switch to autopilot and go on with our daily life, completely unaware of how we are impacting the world around us. We frequently create an unconscious existence where it appears that someone else is running the show.

Summoning the energy to react with intention becomes increasingly difficult, and our instinctive reactions become the norm. In an attempt to survive, we sacrifice our ability to influence the world with directed intention. Over time, many of us lose sight of who we were born to be. In essence, we choose to settle.

Awareness is the key to creating everything we want in our life. Through awareness we begin to ask questions. Where did we come from? Why are we here? Where do we want to go? What do we want to do? Why do we do the things we do? How do we influence in a way that we can be proud of? How do we live a life of intention rather than a life of servitude?

As we ask these questions, the answers follow. Our curiosity ultimately brings us an understanding of who we are and where we came from. It may seem trivial to dig into our past, but the stories of our past become so engrained in our psyche that they subconsciously run our lives. Without intervention, our past takes control of the present and our shadows dictate every choice. We end up going through our entire life on autopilot, so our past becomes our present and our future.

As we begin to understand our stories, we discover roadblocks that have been holding us back our whole lives. We have been working around roadblocks such as denial, distraction, blame, and fear for years, completely unaware of the life that we could be creating for ourselves.

The good news is that we have the power to smash through

any roadblock at a moment's notice. A growing awareness opens the door for the creation of intentions. These intentions have the power to shift our lives from the inside out. When this shift occurs, we are never the same. Once the fire of awareness and intention has been lit, there is no turning back. Roadblocks become speed bumps, shadows become friends, and the life we have always dreamed about becomes a reality.

If we are lucky enough to wake up and realize our power, we begin a journey. It's a journey with twists and turns, struggle and triumph, ups and downs, joy and sorrow. This journey brings with it a great responsibility, but it also brings the freedom of choice, contentment, fulfillment, fortitude, and resiliency. Ultimately, this journey allows us to find our true self so we can tap into our amazing power and change our world with intention.

The clouds that hang over our head extend beyond the horizon of our own life. Fortunately, the rays of sunshine from our soul also extend past the horizon of our life. Don't kid yourself; you are powerful! The intention of this book is to emphasize the fact that we all change the world without making a singular effort on any of our parts. Rather than mindlessly racing toward the finish line with our head down, wreaking havoc as we plow through life, we have a duty to do everything we can to impact the world with directed intention.

This book is a challenge. A challenge to get us all thinking about what our role is, in our own lives and the lives of everyone around us. A challenge to admit that we can all do it better. A challenge to understand who we are as we find our place in this world. A challenge to start showing compassion to ourselves and everyone around us. A challenge for us to get up and change our life and the lives of everyone around us.

As you read this book, I ask that you take a journey with me. Keep an open mind, and create some space to self-explore. This is your life in our world. It's time for us all to do our part to be the best version of ourselves.

It's time!

PART I

PERSPECTIVE

*"We must be the change that we
wish to see in the world."*

—Mahatma Gandhi

SIR ISAAC NEWTON was one of this world's greatest minds. He was the first person to state that every action has an equal and opposite reaction. This was a revolutionary idea at the time, and the concept is still taught in our science classrooms today. Our teachers remind us that he is highly regarded as a genius and a brilliant physicist. And while I would wholeheartedly agree, there is one thing they forget to tell us in science class. Sir Isaac Newton is human, and he is completely full of shit!

Yep, that's right, I just said that Isaac Newton was full of shit. But that's OK, because we all are. I am also full of shit, and so are you. Hold on, don't close the book yet! Stick with me here. I promise that I am going somewhere with all of this.

While I think we can agree that Sir Isaac Newton had an amazing scientific mind, he also had deficiencies, imperfections, weaknesses, and fears. And that is OK. Although I have never met him, I can imagine a time in his life when he had to dig deep, really deep, in an attempt to answer a question that he was completely clueless about. Perhaps in lieu of saying "I don't know," he simply rattled off something he knew sounded good, but in reality his answer was simply full of shit. Who knows? He may have even laughed to himself all the while. Yes, he had an amazing scientific mind, but that doesn't equate to perfection. He was just doing the best he could with what he had been given, and in the end that is all any of us can do.

The reality is that Sir Isaac Newton had no need to be perfect or all-knowing in order to change the world.

Deficiencies and all, he changed the world. His success was ultimately a result of his dedication to working on something that brought meaning to his life. Through awareness and an intention to become the best version of himself, he tapped into his God-given power (which we all have) and in turn, he was simply able to make his shit smell … just a little bit nicer.

Here is the bottom line. Being full of shit isn't a bad thing; it's a human thing. I have a hunch that you may even see hints that I am full of shit as you read my story in the next chapter. None of us will ever really know what the heck we are doing. We are all trying to figure it out as we go. Where's the fun in having it all figured out, anyway?

That is not to say that just because we don't have all the answers, we can't change the world for the better. The reality is that we are not just full of shit. We are actually full of "it." All of "it." We are full of love, joy, heartbreak, shadow, happiness, pain, joy, passion, laziness, inspiration, alignment, confusion, sadness, drive, ego, judgment, blame, responsibility, desire, loathing, hatred, fear, failure, power, and success. Ultimately, we are full of everything that makes life amazing and full of everything that makes life challenging. We are full of all of IT.

Even though we all come from different backgrounds, cultures, and families, we all understand the emotions of being human. Our emotions are universal truths, and they ultimately connect us. We have the power to tap into them at any moment. The key to unlocking our tremendous power lies in our ability to pick and choose when to leverage these parts of ourselves. Of course, this opportunity arises only through awareness.

Without awareness, our emotions and our choices are dictated to us by our past experiences. Sometimes we need anger. Sometimes we need courage. Sometimes we need dedication. Sometimes we need joy. Awareness gives us the power of choice, which in turn allows us to intentionally influence the world. Once we become aware and ultimately accept that we are flawed, our mind opens and the fact that we don't have it all figured out is perfectly fine. This realization opens the door for us to discover our roadblocks, and it becomes the conduit for creativity and lightheartedness. It ultimately lays the groundwork for creating the power of choice.

Writing this book has been a tremendous blessing, but it has not come without many challenges. While writing this book, I have learned how full of shit I really am. I pretend to have it all figured out sometimes. I lose my cool sometimes. I learn lessons the hard way sometimes. I put these words on the page, and while I hope they impact the world in a positive way, let's not kid ourselves. I don't have it all figured out either. I am simply doing the best I can to tap into my own God-given power in an attempt to make the world a better place. I don't have to be perfect to do that. However, I do have to try, and I have to be aware of who I am, where I am, and what I want to create.

This book is intended to remind you that you have that same power. You have pieces within you that bring tremendous power and pieces that hold you back from reaching your true potential. You already have everything you need to change the world and create the life you desire. It's been within you for your entire life. Start asking the questions. What shit is keeping you from bringing forth what you really want? What stories are holding you back from reaching your full potential? What pieces of yourself have you been ignoring? My hope is that, as you read this book, you are able to bring forth the awareness to discover and tap into your own unique "it."

So … if one of the greatest minds of all time is full of it, what does that say about you and me? It says that while we aren't perfect, we are full of unimaginable potential and we have the power to change the world. We just have to try. Let's get out there and change the world together!

CHAPTER 1

JOHN'S STORY

"Every time you are tempted to react in the same old way, ask if you want to be a prisoner of the past or a pioneer of the future."

—Deepak Chopra

THIS FICTIONAL STORY is an example of how energy we put out to the world can have a wide-ranging effect on another person even if we don't know the other person, touch the other person, or even directly connect with the other person. John is meant to exemplify our ability to change our world through awareness combined with a conscious effort to act with intention.

This story could be about any one of us. Just like you and

me, John impacts his world every moment of every day. Just like you and me, he is full of it. His words are powerful, but his energy and presence are more powerful than any words. Just like you and me, John has choices to make and those choices have very real consequences (both good and bad). John's story is a representation of what it means to be human and what it means to be an intentional world changer.

ACT I

John is a hard-working husband, dedicated father of two, and talented financial planner. His business is flourishing, and he has a nice house in a suburb of a growing metropolitan city. As he lies in bed shortly after awaking on Monday morning, he grabs his phone and digs into his email. He immediately notices an email from Robert.

Robert is an old friend and a long-time client—one of John's most important clients, in fact. Robert is furious. The email states that communication has been poor between them and he is very disappointed in the way his account has been handled. When John gets to the end, his heart drops as he sees the words he was hoping weren't there. Robert is moving all his accounts to a different firm. This isn't the first client to leave recently. Robert is one in a series of clients that have packed up and left. John feels sick as he realizes he totally dropped the ball. And this one really hurts. He begins to recognize the ramifications of this situation. This is *bad* news!

John begins to run ideas through his mind about how this happened. He has a new assistant, and the training has been slow-moving; he has been traveling a lot lately; there is always something going on with the family; and his attention has been spread thin. Suffice it to say, things have been crazy lately. He can't believe he let this fall through the cracks.

LET'S STOP THERE FOR A MOMENT and assess what's happening. First of all, this client has written this email, probably from a place of frustration, anger, and maybe even a place of ego. *You hurt me ... we were friends and you treated me bad. So, my revenge is to hurt you or your business.* John is taking in all this information, processing it, drawing conclusions, and making plans on how to move forward. His physical body is reacting. His heart "dropped," which means that his heart is feeling stress and his blood pressure is rising. His stomach muscles are tightening, his teeth are grinding, and his adrenaline is pumping. His whole world is now wrapped up in this situation. His negative emotions begin to take over.

Whether he knows it or not, John has a choice. Here he stands at a crossroad, which will affect many people. This moment, right now, *will* change the world one way or another. At this moment, he has to ask himself a question. How is he going to react? He may ask this question consciously or unconsciously, but this question is asked one way or the other.

John's subconscious takes over and he knows he can't just stay in bed all day wallowing in self-pity. He has to get up and get moving on this, now! At this particular moment, John doesn't have the energy to try to withhold his true emotions. He is angry and ashamed about his mistakes. He begins to contemplate the way things "should" be.

John heads downstairs. As his wife turns around to wish him a good morning, John looks over and says, "Yeah, great morning," with more than just a hint of sarcasm.

"Are you OK?"

"Not really," he responds. "Everything is a complete mess. Robert is really mad and is moving all his accounts to another firm. He is blaming everything on me and says that I don't communicate with him. That's garbage! I communicate with him all the time. Whatever, I don't have time to talk about it right now. I have to get to work so I can sort all of this out."

JOHN'S NEGATIVE ENERGY has just rubbed off on his wife, who is now carrying some of John's stress and anxiety. How will her new mood rub off on the kids, her friends, or her co-workers? She was happy before they interacted, but now she is concerned for John. She also knows he is going to be upset when he gets home. Now, she will take that heavy energy with her into the world as she interacts with everyone and everything.

After talking with his wife, John storms upstairs and begins getting ready for the day. As he picks out his clothes, gets dressed, does his hair, and brushes his teeth, he thinks about all the ways that Robert is totally out of line. He runs those words through his head and works to convince himself he is right.

He finishes getting ready at a rapid pace and is ready to head out the door. As he steps out of his room, his waking kids greet him at the top of the stairs. "Hi, Daddy. Good morning."

"Good morning," he replies quickly. He gives them a cold hug and kiss and then says, "I'll see you both later. I have to go now."

Neither of his kids knows what's going on with Dad or why he is upset. All they know is that Dad is mad and has to go ... again.

HOW LONG DID THE INTERACTION with his kids last? Ten seconds, maybe? Could this interaction affect them for the day? Definitely. For a lifetime? Possibly, especially if it happens on regular basis. Kids will shape a worldview based on interactions with their parents. So it makes sense that they may begin to feel they are not important, or that Daddy loves work more than me, or that work has to be a struggle, or that the world is a hostile place, and so on. During this short interaction, John is very inward-focused. He is worried about his own problems. He has no ill will toward his kids, and he may even be trying to protect them by not saying anything about the problem. In his mind, he is justified to be short with his wife and kids, because he "has a lot on his mind." They shouldn't have to take on any of it, and they need to understand that he has a lot on his plate.

Regardless of reality, how much of that story do young children understand? Probably not much. Because they lack the wisdom to analyze what is really happening, they make the interaction about themselves. They can't hear the inner dialogue going on in John's head. They don't understand the complexities of the situation. They do understand that Dad was upset and didn't give them the time they truly desire. They begin their own attempt to figure out what is happening and what this scenario means about them. They may think to themselves, "Poor Daddy. I need to take better care of him." They may think, "What did I do to make Dad so mad that he just leaves without saying goodbye?" They may associate his behavior with how they are supposed to show up in the world. In other words, they may say, "Oh, this is how I am supposed to deal with my problems."

John heads downstairs and gives a quick kiss goodbye to his wife as he essentially blows past her on his way out the door. As he hops in his car, he has a mixture of emotions that range from frustration, shame, anger, panic, and tension. Now it's time to get into the office.

He stops at the local coffee shop so he can grab his morning cup. As he rigidly stands in line, he is sure to avoid eye contact with anyone. He doesn't want any small talk today. *Just give me a cup of coffee and get me on my way*, he thinks. Finally, he gets to the front of the line.

"What can I get you this morning?" a friendly voice asks from behind the counter.

"Triple shot of espresso," John replies.

Wearing a bright smile, and noticing that John has not been having a great morning, the barista tries to lighten the mood by making a little joke. "Oh, wow! Triple shot! Someone must be having a slow morning. Time for a pick-me-up, huh?" he says with a slight grin on his face.

"Yes," John answers in a short tone. "It's been a rough morning, and I just want my coffee."

"Oh, I see," the barista says. His smile quickly fades as he notices that his lighthearted joke fell flat.

WHILE JOHN'S COMMENT WAS A LITTLE RUDE, the energy he brought had a much bigger impact. Additionally, John's attitude had absolutely nothing to do with the barista. However, as humans, we always try to make sense of our interactions with the world. So naturally, the barista assumes some responsibility for John's attitude. He may feel bad for trying to make a joke, or he may get upset because people are rude. Thoughts start to creep into the barista's head. Maybe he should just take the orders and keep everything professional. People don't like his stupid jokes anyway, so he might as well not risk the pain of falling on his face when he tries to brighten someone's day.

People can be jerks anyway, so why bother to be nice? If people are just going to treat him like that when he tries to make them smile, then he'll stop trying.

In reality, the barista did nothing wrong, but one way or the other he has absorbed John's negativity. His energy has decreased, and now he is simply looking to get through the day without any more risk. He is no longer looking for opportunities to make people laugh and smile. He is looking to protect himself. How might the barista's new attitude affect all the people he talks to today? How might John's negative energy affect other people who were simply standing in the line next to him?

John leaves the coffee shop and continues his journey to the office. Lamenting as he drives, he continues to ponder as he merges onto the interstate and heads downtown. He thinks about how Robert is totally in the wrong here, and he worries about how the conversation with Robert is going to play out. Suddenly, he is shaken from his mindless trance as another car merges onto the highway right in front of him. John didn't even notice this guy, and he nearly clipped John's front bumper as he began to merge. "What the hell!" he yells.

Time to redirect some anger and frustration onto this jerk!

"Hey, don't worry about me! Come right on in!" he yells as he rides right up on the other car's bumper.

He sees an opening in the next lane over and aggressively moves over to pass this guy. As he drives past, he yells and throws up his hands, making sure this guy knows that he is not OK with what just happened. As he looks over, he notices that the driver is not a guy after all. It's a lady, maybe forty-five or so. He can tell that his anger is landing and she is taken aback by his actions. *That's right*, he thinks. *That'll teach her.* "Learn to drive or get off the road!" he yells, as he cuts right in front of her car.

JOHN, whether he likes it or not, has thrown negative energy into the world, and it was absorbed by the other driver. There is no way to know exactly how this negative energy is going to show up with this other person, but more than likely, it will exacerbate some kind of negative loop that she runs in her own life.

See, what John failed to realize is that the driver of that other car was in deep thought about her own life. She hadn't even noticed John until after he was riding on her tail. She was totally caught up in her own life story. She is currently going through a divorce, and was thinking about her kids and how much she would miss them if she loses custody. Already feeling vulnerable, she is very shaken as John drives by, shouting and throwing blame on her. As he cuts her off, she begins to cry. She thinks about how mean and unfair the world is. Why even try anymore? Maybe she should just give up. She then takes this energy into her work. She tries to cover it up, but everyone can tell she has been crying, and they want to know what is going on.

Now her co-workers commiserate with her, and the negative vibrations reverberate throughout the office. Was John's intention to ruin this woman's day? Was his intention to lower the energy of her entire office? Not really, but he is a world changer.

Finally, he arrives at the office and is greeted by his assistant. She is just getting settled and has no idea what is happening with their biggest account.

"Good morning, John," she says.

"Hi," he snips.

Sensing that something is definitely going on here, she asks, "Is everything OK?"

"No! Robert is moving his accounts, traffic is awful, I'm exhausted…"

"Wait, Robert is leaving?"

"Yes, he says that we haven't been communicating well and he feels like we aren't representing him well."

As he looks at his assistant, he realizes that she really should have been communicating with Robert more frequently as well. This is as much her fault as it was his own. He can't do everything!

Without warning, he sternly addresses her, "Why haven't you been calling him every Monday? I can't do everything around here, and I depend on you to help me with this kind of thing." He continues, "Whatever! I'll figure it out."

He storms off without giving his assistant an opportunity to defend herself. As she sits back down, she is feeling defeated and unmotivated. Then she begins to think about this interaction. *I don't remember missing any emails. Maybe this is my fault. Wait a minute. No! I return all phone calls and emails. This is his business and his client. This is his fault. I can't believe he would treat me like that. I do so much for him and then he treats me like that. I don't have to take this!*

And on and on the conversation in her head goes.

NOT EVEN 9 A.M. and John has changed the world yet again, unintentional or not. His assistant had come into the office with a positive attitude. However, after this interaction, she is feeling defeated and angry. When her co-workers talk to her, they can tell she is upset. As the story is relayed, her co-workers commiserate with her. This isn't the first time this has happened in their office, and now the conversation begins to shift to discussions about whether any of them should continue to take this. Maybe it's time to start looking for another place to work. Just like what happened with the lady in the car, the overall energy of the entire office is lowered. John's negative energy has passed from him, to his assistant, and then to others in the office. Rather than focusing on how to solve an urgent problem in a way that could benefit everyone, the people in the office begin to consider how to get revenge, how to support their position *against* their bosses, and how to run away. Creativity is closed off, and resentment and anger take over.

Perhaps this isn't the best energy for a functional office.

What a day, right? Have you ever had a day like that? Perhaps you have, and even though you are well aware that you are losing control and acting in a way that you are not proud of, you continue anyway. Your emotions get the best of you, and reaction becomes the driving force. By the end of the day, you are exhausted and completely out of control.

As much as I don't like to admit it, I definitely have been there. This story is not an actual scenario from my life, but it very well could be. While scenarios like this still show up in my life from time to time, I have found that the more I dig, and the more I look inward, the more aware I become. As my awareness grows, my intentions become more clear. Then my actions begin to align with the person I desire to be, and ultimately I experience these rough scenarios less and less.

Remember that perfection is not the goal. The simple act of attempting to do it better is all it takes to impact the world in a positive way.

ACT II

Let's shift gears a bit and look at this same story again, but now John is coming from a different place. In this scenario, John has been self-exploring and has created a conscious vision for himself. He has set daily intentions around his anger. He has been seeing a coach for some time and has made self-reflection a part of his daily life. He is not perfect by any means, but he sincerely tries every day to be the best version of himself.

Once again, our story begins with John lying in bed. Through his work with his coach, John knows that looking at his phone in bed is the worst way to start his day. Rather than letting the outside world influence his day right off the bat, he sits in bed for fifteen minutes and reflects on his intentions for the day. He sits quietly as he runs a few questions through his mind:

- How do I want to *be* today?
- How do I want to show up today?
- How do I want my interactions to look and feel today?
- How do I want my energy to flow out into the world today?

After a few minutes of centering reflection, he goes downstairs. His wife turns around to wish him a good morning. John leans over as he gives her a quick kiss on the cheek.

"How is your morning?" she asks.

"Great," he replies. "I'm going to head downstairs and do my meditation."

As John heads downstairs, he checks to make sure his phone is not in his pocket. He likes to make sure he can focus without interruptions. He knows he can check his phone later.

THE ACTUAL SITUATION has not changed. There is still an email in John's inbox that he's going to have to deal with. It is still bad news. However, through his intentional routine, he has already created a very different interaction with his wife and has planted a seed in his day that will positively impact anyone he connects with.

After thirty minutes or so, John finishes his morning routine. He is feeling centered and ready to attack the day. He has an intention set and feels prepared to handle any obstacles that come his way. Now he is ready to step into his home office to check his email. Just like before, he reads the email from Robert, and his heart drops. And just like before, this really hurts and John feels sick as he realizes that he totally dropped the ball. This is *bad* news!

JOHN HAS RECEIVED the exact same email. The exact same information has been presented. He immediately recognizes the importance of this situation, and his first response is still, "Uh-oh!" He is still taken aback and still runs stories through his mind. His heart still sinks, he still worries about how this could have happened, and he still feels the stress of the situation. He is now at the same crossroad where he must make a choice. Given this bad news, how does he intend to show up today?

Almost immediately, John becomes aware that his face is getting hot, his stomach is in knots, his heart is beating fast, and he is starting to "ramp up." He has seen this before and knows what happens when he allows this automatic reaction to completely take over. He knows he has to make a choice, and he knows he has to regroup before he can think clearly. On this particular morning, his self-awareness is already paying dividends. He pushes back from his desk and closes his eyes. He knows that the first step to clearing his mind is to feel his emotions fully, so he gives himself permission to get pissed. He tenses his body, clinches his fists, pulls his shirt over his mouth, and yells under his breath as loud as he can, "AHHHHHHHHHHH!" *How the hell did I allow this to happen?* he thinks to himself as he releases all his frustration. He continues like this for a few moments until he has released this negative energy. He pulls his shirt off of his mouth, takes a few deep breaths, and on the last big exhale, he lets out an audible sigh.

Now, he sits back, closes his eyes and begins to clear his mind. He forgets about the issue at hand and focuses on the intention he set for himself earlier. "How do I want to *be* today?" He continues to focus on how he wants to show up in the world. After about five minutes, he has released the negative energy and is refocused.

ONCE AGAIN, there is still a big issue that must be addressed. The difference is that John has made a conscious decision about how he will *be* today. He has recentered himself and created space to experience his emotions. He has not forgotten and he has not ignored the importance of the issue at hand. He has simply used his tools to ground himself, clear his mind, and prepare himself to make choices that are aligned with his intention.

Time to address this issue. He needs to get dressed, get into the office, and find a way to make this right with Robert. No time to sit here anymore. Time to go. He hurries upstairs.

He nearly forgets to say hi to his kids. Luckily, they catch him at the top of the stairs.

"Hi, Daddy!" they both say.

At this moment, his adrenaline is pumping. His first instinct is to simply say hi, give them a quick hug, and then be on his way. After all, he has important things to attend to.

Suddenly, he becomes aware of this inclination and reflects on his intention. He takes a moment to collect his thoughts. He knows it's important for his kids and himself to connect before he leaves. He stops, gets down on one knee, looks them both in the eyes and says, "Good morning? How did you sleep last night?"

"Good," they both say.

"Great. I love to hear that. I love you guys. So, listen, I just received an important message from work, and I have to get into the office right away. I am sorry that I have to leave so quickly, but I want you guys to know that I love you and I hope you have a great day! Can I have a quick hug before I go?"

His kids give him a quick hug and say, "I love you too. Have a great day!"

JOHN'S MORNING ROUTINE created a framework for his day that allowed him to shift almost instantly when he noticed that he wasn't in alignment with his intention. John was able to compartmentalize work issues and his relationship with his kids. Notice that he was able to adjust in an instant as he recognized his instinctual response to blow past the kids. Even though he is still in a rush, his interaction didn't take any longer and didn't "cost" him anything extra compared to his interaction in the previous scenario. Additionally, rather than having a short-lived and unexplained interaction, his kids now have an idea of what is going on. They now recognize that "Daddy has to get to work to fix a problem, because that is what Daddy does at work." They can now make their story about Daddy's work rather than about how Daddy is mad or upset at them. The kids are no longer tapped into John's energy. Kids are very resilient and in this scenario, they have already sloughed off the interaction as they head downstairs with their usual childlike enthusiasm, ready to enjoy their day. There is no telling how his children's energy may now impact the world today. Perhaps this energy is transferred to their mom or a fellow student who is struggling.

John heads downstairs, looks his wife in the eyes, and says, "I'm sorry, but I have to rush out. I have a work issue with Robert, and I need to deal with it ASAP. Sorry that I have to run so quickly, but I hope you have a great day. I will explain later. OK?"

"Yes, of course," she says. "I'll get the kids to school. Good luck! Love you."

"Thank you, and I love you too."

HIS WIFE is still disappointed that John is having a tough morning. She is still disappointed that he had to run out so quickly. However, the pill is a bit easier to swallow this time since John took the time (a few extra seconds) to check in and let her know what is going on. As she moves through her day, she is not influenced by a sour interaction with her husband. She is vibrating at a higher energy. She is more prepared to approach the day from a place of peace and positivity. There is no telling how his wife's energy may impact the world today. Perhaps her confidence rubs off on another mom who needs a boost of self-esteem.

John hops in his car as a mixture of emotions that range from frustration, shame, anger, panic, and tension pour over him. However, this time all those emotions are curbed by an inner knowing that he can handle this situation and he will work it out, one way or another.

As he drives, he keeps telling himself to relax. "I've got this," he says to himself over and over. However, it just doesn't seem to alleviate his stress and negativity. Then he remembers a tool his coach taught him. In an instant, he knows what he has to do. Feel it completely ... again!

He takes a moment, focuses on all the negativity, feels it in his bones, and lets it all out as he drives. He clenches his body, yells, and throws a fit. His face gets red, his blood pressure rises, and he gets a kink in his neck. He feels his frustration and anger fully, and places no judgment on himself. This takes only about ten seconds. Then, without a conscious thought, he hears himself let out a huge sigh. His body begins to relax, his breathing slows, his blood pressure begins to drop, and he settles into the moment. A few more deep breaths and almost instantly he's ready to refocus on how to correct this fixable issue. *I've got this. Let's figure this out.*

JOHN HAS NO IDEA why this works and it doesn't really matter. In the end, all that matters is that he is back on track and ready to attack the issue. Anger and frustration are just feelings, and it is perfectly fine and perhaps even therapeutic to experience these feelings. After all, feelings are not inherently good or bad; they just *are*. Sometimes we need anger and frustration in our life.

Once we understand that it is OK to feel emotions, we can become friends with them and use them when needed. Anger and frustration are not our enemies. Leveraged properly, they can actually be some of our greatest allies. When John takes the time to experience his emotions rather than making up a story about how he shouldn't feel this way, he is free to work in tandem with his emotions. In essence, he validates his true feelings through acknowledgment. That sigh he lets out is a natural reaction for many of us when we really let something go. That is John's moment of transformation. Now he is refocused on what his next moves are rather than focusing on the problems themselves. There is no predicting how this shift will show up as John interacts with people throughout the day.

John decides to stop at the local coffee shop so he can grab his morning cup. As he stands in line, he is thinking about the best approach to talk to Robert. He runs ideas through his mind about how he is going to *be* when they talk. He thinks about what he can say and how he can say it most effectively. After all, his intention is to keep Robert as a client and make things right. It's never too late.

As he approaches the counter, the barista asks in a friendly voice, "What can I get you this morning?"

"Hello. A triple shot of espresso would work wonders."

Wearing a slight grin on his face, and noticing that John needs a little boost, the barista tries to lighten the mood by making a little joke. "Oh, wow! Triple shot! Someone must have a big day! Time for a pick-me-up, huh?" he says.

"You have no idea," John says with a smile. "Challenging morning for sure, but nothing I can't handle. Of course, a solid cup of coffee always helps!"

"Yes it does," the barista says as he in the order.

WHETHER JOHN REALIZES it or not, he has put a powerful energy out into the world in this simple inter-action. The people in the line can feel his confidence and power. He has an aura that people can sense. Just as in the last scenario, the barista puts himself out there, not knowing how this person will respond. When John banters back, he sets an example of what it looks like for a person to have a rough morning and still keep his composure. Unbeknownst to John, he has reinforced an idea within the barista that there are people who can take tough situations in stride. There has been an ever-so-slight shift in the barista that builds confidence within him that he, too, can handle challenging customers. He feels more confident, and he feels validated. John's positive energy has created the potential to propagate through the barista and the people in line next to him.

John leaves the coffee shop and continues his journey to the office. As he sits in his car, he drifts back to his thoughts. He gets that sinking in his gut as he recalls the email and remembers the conversation he has to have with Robert. Suddenly he catches himself. He takes a deep breath, lets it out with a sigh, and reminds himself that, no matter the outcome, everything will work out the way it's supposed to. He is suddenly shaken from his thoughts as another car merges onto the highway right in front of him and nearly hits him. "Whoa!" he says in a surprised voice. His first inclination is to give this guy a piece of his mind. However, that feeling is short-lived, because his real focus is on his intention to make things right with Robert. He feels centered, and it's going to take more than a careless driver to knock him off his game right now. He simply allows the experience to be what it is and then goes back to his thoughts about how he wants to *be* today as he enters his office.

HERE WE HAVE an interesting concept about how John has changed the world by addition through subtraction. When he was cut off, he had a choice. He could let it go or he could get revenge. If John lets it go, that person can go on with their day without any confrontation from their mistake. By letting it go, he has changed the world for the better. By letting it go and by not lowering the energy of the world through revenge, he has added to the energy of the world in a positive way. He may have been justified to "teach this person a lesson," but he decided to put his energy into more productive thought processes.

He finally arrives at the office and is greeted by his assistant. "Good morning," he replies. "How was your evening?" His voice is stern, but still friendly.

"It was good. Thank you for asking. I see you have a few meetings today, and I received your email about those documents I need to send out to a few of your clients. Anything else on the agenda for today?"

"Well," he says in a somber, yet confident tone, "Robert is upset and we need to do damage control. He's pretty mad, so we need to do whatever we can to make this right"

"Oh, no! He is our biggest client. What happens if he leaves?"

"Don't worry about that. It'll work out. Whether he leaves or stays, our business will be better because of all of this. With that said, we will do everything we can to keep him here."

"What can I do to help?" she asks.

As John internalizes this question, it dawns on him that his assistant has played a fairly substantial role in this. There is a system in place, and she didn't follow protocol, which ultimately led to many of the complaints from Robert. He recognizes that he gets to make a choice about how to handle this situation. There are a lot of options, but ultimately, he decides that now is not the time to confront his assistant. He just needs to get the workday started. "For right now, please hold my calls and get started on the items you just mentioned. We will touch base once I get more info, and we will go from there. Sound good?"

ONCE AGAIN, we see addition by subtraction. John knows full well that his assistant played a role. Her systems are less than perfect and she needs to dial them in if they are to keep clients happy. But he also knows that as the leader, he must take full responsibility for this problem. By refusing to let his frustration with his assistant take control, and by letting this issue slide for the time being, he keeps his assistant motivated and keeps the energy at a higher level in the office. This is not to say that he will not address the issue with her. He is simply waiting for the appropriate time so he can address the more immediate issue at hand. He will address the growth opportunity for his assistant with a more skilled and intentional approach later. In this case, he has set an example for how to approach a challenging situation. Anyone involved in this issue now has an example of how to look at a challenging situation and approach it from a place of power. They can take this experience and apply it to all types of different scenarios in their own lives. Now this positive energy will continue to propagate throughout the world.

Additionally, when the time comes, his assistant will be much more open to hearing John's message about her mistakes. His careful thought will lead to a much more constructive conversation. Once his assistant realizes her role, she will have an opportunity to learn from her mistakes and become a better person and employee. Once again, these lessons have the potential to change her world, her interactions with others, and the world at large in ways that are completely unmeasurable.

THE MORAL

We could continue with this story as it propagates through many people's lives, for days, weeks, months, years, or generations. Our smallest interactions start chain reactions that can amplify as they influence the world. Our energy or words may make the barista say, "I hate this job, and I will never serve food again." Is that a good thing or a bad thing? Our attitude may make the assistant question why she is still in this dead-end job.

Is that a good thing or a bad thing? Our disengagement with our kids may make them question whether they are good or bad. Is that a good thing or a bad thing?

Have you ever made a call to your phone company and the person on the other end of the phone says, "Hi. How are you doing today?" in a very upbeat and happy way? Have you ever made that call and the person on the other end of the phone says, "Hi. How are you doing today?" in a tired and annoyed voice? Did you feel your emotions shift just a little in either of these circumstances? If the answer is yes, then you understand my point.

Every moment of every day, you have a choice. Should you relent to people's negative energy and follow them, or should you lead and intentionally influence? Should you put on a fake smile and humor them? Should you copy them? Should you give them a taste of their own medicine?

That is what this book is all about. This book is all about the idea that we influence other people whether we like it or not. So, as fellow humans who are all just trying to figure out this whole life thing, let's ask the all-important question: How do we *intentionally* influence the energy of the world with a conscious effort that comes from a place of power and authenticity?

IS IT EVEN POSSIBLE?

It's impossible to tell exactly *how* our daily interactions change the complicated web that is our world, but our energy and our interactions *do* in fact change it. My challenge to you is for you to remember that you are powerful. When we string together enough little positive shifts, we can create massive world changes that propagate down the line in ways we never dreamed possible. We may not solve every world problem, but by intentionally shifting our energy, we absolutely can impact the world in amazing ways. Nelson Mandela once said, "It always seems impossible until it's done."

How do you intend to change the world today?

Really let that question sink in, and give it some thought. How do you intend to change the world today?

CHAPTER 2

OUR STORIES

*"I don't like that man. I must get
to know him better."*

—Abraham Lincoln

I CAN ONLY ASSUME that Honest Abe was talking about a man "out there," but this is just as pertinent to the man or woman that resides within us.

If we want to change the world with intention, we must first know who we are and why we are the way we are. Developing a true understanding of ourselves begins by creating an understanding of our personal story. How can we get where we want to go and create the life we want if we don't know where we are right now? Through an understanding of our past experiences, we gain a more clear understanding of our strengths, our weaknesses, our commitments, our desires, our shadows, and our programs. Only through self-reflection can we discover our most authentic self, which ultimately allows us to tap into our power and leverage all of ourselves to get us where we want to go.

It may be a little counterintuitive, but we must look back in order to move forward. We must figure out where we came from to figure out where we are now. Only then can we create an intentional plan to move forward.

I liken this concept to being blindfolded and dropped into the middle of a forest with no idea where we are on the map. If we want to navigate, first we have to slow down, observe, and make inferences about where we currently reside. Once we know where we are on the map, we can then begin to formulate a plan about how to get where we intend to go. If we rush forward, crumple up the map, and acquiesce to the idea that discovering our place on the map is a hopeless waste of time, then we begin moving in random directions. Through blind luck, we may find our destination, but in reality, it's much more likely that we will end up walking in circles, becoming ever more confused, lost, and frustrated.

Many of us use our limited time on this earth trying to figure out how to get to some ambiguous destination, moving without any idea about where we came from, how we got where we are, and with no real intention. Like a robot, going through the motions, devoid of passion and purpose. Eventually these feelings often lead to depression, anger, alcoholism, blame, fear, pain, broken marriages, broken relationships with friends, broken relationships with children, lack of fulfillment, despair, shadows, or victimhood. Does any of this sound familiar? As you will see when you read my story in a few pages, some of these conditions were commonplace in my life. That is not living. That is an empty existence.

WHAT IS SHADOW?

Before we get to deep into this chapter, I want to touch on the idea of "shadows." I go into more detail about shadows in chapter 3; for now, we need only a basic description. Shadows are pieces of ourselves or of our psyche that we disown or pretend don't exist. Shadows are sometimes referred to as "programs." There is a distinction between the two, but we will get to that later. Perhaps as a child we had an experience and our brain created a story around that event. The story we created served us well during that time in our life, so the program became more engrained. Eventually the story became so engrained that our subconscious taps into it frequently and we run on autopilot. This happens whether the original program is still serving us or not. This program has now become a habit that we are completely unaware of.

We all have moments in our life that make our hearts smile with pride. These are the stories we love sharing with friends while we laugh hysterically. On the other end of the spectrum, we have stories that we hide. We don't share these shameful stories with anyone. We simply bury them. We believe they don't drive any aspect of our life. Well, I am about to lay a hard truth on you. These negative/challenging stories sit in the background of our subconscious and absolutely run our lives, whether we like it or not. Denying a truth doesn't make it any less true. These moments are a part of us, and they shape our psyche. When we suffer trauma, we create self-defining conclusions about who we are. We are not good enough, strong enough, smart enough, qualified enough, tall enough, pretty enough, and so on. These are our shadows, and we use them to create stories in an attempt to protect ourselves from future harm, and we refer back to them when we make life choices.

The positive stories are great and I would love to focus on those all the time, but the fact of the matter is the positive stories do not carry the same opportunities for growth. Don't get me wrong; we need our happy, healthy, and funny stories. They serve a valuable purpose. What I am saying is that if the objective is to grow, we have to crawl back into the depths of our subconscious and dig up all the raw, dirty, and painful stories of our past. We need to embrace our dark side and make friends with our shadows. We need to accept that we are human and we have made mistakes, many of which hurt others and many more that have hurt ourselves. We need to understand and accept that people have wronged us and hurt us.

Richard Rohr said in his amazing book, *Falling Upward*, "Somewhere in my late forties, I realized that many people loved me for who I was not. And many people resented me and rejected me for who I was not. Conversely, many of you loved me for who I am, warts and all, and this was the only love that ever redeemed me." If true love and acceptance is the only love that redeems, then doesn't it make sense that we learn to love ourselves, warts and all?

Until we look at the warts of our psyche, how can we truly love ourself through and through? By digging into our past and pulling away the layers of the onion, we can begin to forgive ourselves, we can begin to forgive those who have wronged us, and most importantly, we can begin to love ourselves again—just like we did when we first entered this world. This work is the beginning. This is how we find out where we are on the map so we can begin our journey through the forest toward our true calling.

It's time for us to look our demons right in the eyes and address them head-on. FDR said it very well: "The only thing we have to fear is fear itself."

One of my favorite quotes from Marianne Williamson states, "Our deepest fear is not that we are inadequate. Our deepest fear is that we are powerful beyond measure. It is our light, not our darkness, that most frightens us."

It's extremely difficult to evaluate ourselves with honesty and tenderness, and that is why so few people are willing to do what it takes to create meaningful change in their life. It is difficult to look back at our childhood and relive those moments of pain, anger, and disappointment. It's hard to recall our stories and rewrite them in a way that allows us to take responsibility and move beyond. It's challenging to revisit the people who have wronged us as we look to forgive. Our ego doesn't want any of that. Our ego wants to find evidence that the stories we have created are, and will forever be … right. Our ego wants "them" to be wrong.

In an attempt to protect our fragile ego, we hold onto the anger and the pain that we have stored in our memories, and we lean into that anger and pain as we build our story. Rather than addressing our past and accepting reality, we curl up into an emotional ball and put up impenetrable walls to assure us protection from the dire fate of vulnerability. Now no one can hurt us again, and no one can prove us wrong. This feels safe and secure. Of course, this also guarantees that we will never understand who we really are and, therefore, no one else will ever know who we really are either. It's hard to live a fulfilling life when we do everything we can to hide from ourselves and from the world. The ego likes predictability and the status quo (because it's safe and reassuring), but the soul longs for truth and expansion. Therein lies the rub and the root of what this journey is all about.

FACING OUR SHADOW

While I am not here to promote recklessness, I wholeheartedly believe that none of us can tap into our God-given power by playing it safe and avoiding struggle. Risk creates the opportunity for us to push beyond our imaginary boundaries, and it creates the space for our soul to expand. The only way to truly step into our power is to dare to challenge ourselves and our ego.

The climb to the top of the mountain is full of challenges, but I promise that the view from up there is worth every effort. And while enjoying a safe little nap in the parking lot of the trailhead is comfortable, it also robs us of the amazing journey that ultimately leads us to the majestic beauty that is the mountaintop. As always, the choice is ours to make.

Through self-reflection and a dedication to finding truth, I am working to face my own fears and tap into my personal power. I have learned that the key to moving forward through an understanding of who I really am is found in the process of self-discovery. Sometimes it feels a bit like whining as I go back in time and relive painful moments, but discovery is the first step in the creation of a new, more powerful me.

For most of my life, I thought I understood who I was and where I came from. That was until I made a conscious choice to take the risk and begin digging into my past. Unbeknownst to me, the events of my life defined who I was for many years. They became personal stories that dictated beliefs and in turn directed day-to-day decisions. Thirty years after these events occurred, they completely ran my life. My ego was doing its part to prove my righteousness and to keep me safe, all while I sat in the passenger seat of my own bus.

Once I began to honestly look at how others treated me while I was growing up and how I responded to those life experiences, I was able to take responsibility for the role I play in the creation of my life. This was, and still is, a very challenging and rewarding task. However, only through the process of honest reflection and acceptance of my responsibility have I been able to learn and grow from those experiences.

You will likely see that although the details of our stories differ quite a bit, the way we build our "onion" is fairly similar. In other words, I took in my experiences, used those experiences to attach meaning about myself, created conclusions about who

I am, designed strategies to protect myself, and ultimately built shadows that ran my life.

Below is a synopsis of my journey, and I will go into more details next, but it is meant to exemplify how we are all wounded souls longing to fit in and find our purpose in life. It also shows how we all have the potential for growth, greatness, and fulfillment. We have all felt hurt, let down, frustrated, angry, or upset. If you have felt any of these emotions, then you are wounded too, and that is perfectly human.

Being wounded doesn't mean that we are messed up beyond reclamation. It doesn't mean that there is something inherently wrong with us, and it doesn't mean that we need to look upon ourselves in a negative light. Additionally, being wounded doesn't mean that we need to buy a one-way ticket to the doldrums where we have free rein to lament about what a loser we are. Quite the contrary, through acceptance and understanding of our woundedness, we begin to find our light as we build upon the remains of our tumultuous past. It's time to accept our broken nature for what it is: an opportunity. From the ashes of our woundedness comes the opportunity for growth. As we begin to understand and love our woundedness, our light is released into the world as we tap into our true power.

There once was a boy born in the year of the monkey. He was a goofy boy who didn't care much about fitting in. He would rather lie in the grass and watch clouds pass by than focus on things like success. He felt abused by his peers. He was a rejected boy, full of loneliness and despair. He was a boy whose kind-hearted spirit eventually gave way to negative beliefs about himself and the world. He grew to be a young man who began to distrust others in an effort to protect himself. He was to be a man that understood he was alone in this world. He struggled to fit into a world that didn't want him and didn't understand him. He saw much adversity in his life. He walked to the edge of self-destruction brought on by a lifetime of self-limiting beliefs. He was full of confusion, contradiction, fault, anger, love, pain, success, failure, frustration, and intention. He was a broken soul striving for wholeness. He was a man who would look inward and see the powerful being that lay within. He would become a man who would do the work to become who he wanted to be. He would tap into his power in an effort to become the best version of himself. He would strive to make the world a better place. He would become a beautiful human being who is powerful beyond anyone's wildest dreams.

Because I believe our stories are powerful, I am sharing my story with you. I am also going to ask you to write out your story. My story may be the one here in this book, but all our stories are important. Perhaps by me sharing mine, you will find inspiration to understand and share your own. As you write, please remember that just like our friend, Sir Isaac Newton, we are all full of it!

MY STORY

When I was young, I would say before I was eight years old, I was a pie-in-the-sky, happy-go-lucky kid who wanted only to play with friends and lose myself in thought. I didn't care about what clothes I should wear. I didn't pay much attention to social norms or protecting my inner thoughts. I was very outgoing and simply wanted to express myself as I was. As I interacted with peers in school, I realized that everyone else seemed to have these social norms memorized, and I felt like I was late to the party. By third grade, I learned there was something wrong with me. Why didn't I care about the clothes I wore? What was I supposed to wear so I would fit in? How did everyone else know what was cool and what wasn't cool? Why did everyone look at me weird when I would express a thought composed of truth, honesty, and passion? As confusion set in, my story was beginning to take shape. By sixth grade, it got to a point where any comment I would make to a group of peers was immediately assumed to be weird, wrong, or stupid, and they would use the opportunity to remind me why my thoughts didn't matter.

This was very frustrating, mostly because I was a very active and caring child. I had lots of ideas, and I thought if I just cared for others and remained genuine, my peers would recognize the value I bring to this world. However, it seemed that the exact opposite held true. The more genuine and vulnerable I was, the more I was ridiculed. I didn't know it at the time, but eventually, I created a mask.

The mask I chose to wear in elementary school was anger. I found that through sheer force, I could get others to back down. It got to the point that if anyone said anything I didn't like, I would push them, hit them, or fight them after school. I wasn't afraid to stand up for myself, and I wore that fact as a badge of honor. Unfortunately, this badge of honor led to a near daily defensive routine. I have no idea how many fights

I participated in throughout my childhood, but I do know that by the fourth grade I was fighting on a regular basis. It was just part of life for me.

At this time, I was also dealing with my parents' divorce. I lived with my mom, who was working, going to school, and trying to raise three wild kids. She didn't have much time to hang out with us. For the most part, we were latchkey kids. We didn't have a lot of boundaries with my mom, and we didn't have much time with either parent. We saw my dad only every other weekend, and it seemed that we spent most of our time there cleaning his house or playing on our own outside. Outside the occasional hunting or camping trip, I don't have many vivid memories of shooting hoops, playing catch, or any other quality time with my mom or dad. Neither of my parents seemed to make it a priority to attend my basketball games, and that was hard for me. It made me feel unimportant.

Don't get me wrong; I learned a lot from both my parents. But in those days, it felt like my dad really didn't want me around, and it seemed that my mom just didn't have the time I needed. I received very little positive reinforcement from my dad, and ultimately that made me feel like I had let him down. Rarely was I blessed to have a real heart–to-heart talk with my dad. Yelling after my mistakes seemed more the norm. I felt like I was a disappointment to him. My mom tried to connect with me, but we had such little time together that a true connection was nearly impossible. It wasn't that my mom or dad wanted me to feel bad or unimportant. I know they loved me and just wanted to see me succeed, but the reality was that I was trying to figure out how I fit into the world. I was building a story about myself. It didn't matter how many facts were involved in the creation of these thoughts, because in the end, my story was my truth. And so, this is the truth I lived for much of my childhood.

As I entered middle school, things continued like this. I felt like the only kid in school who had no real friends. Even the nerds had each other. I wasn't a bookworm; I wasn't a band kid. I played basketball but didn't hang out with any teammates. According to them, I didn't even deserve to be on the team.

During eighth grade basketball tryouts, we had quite a few kids come out for the team. I knew there was a lot of competition and I was on the bubble. However, this was the only extracurricular activity I was ever any good at. Not only that, but my brother was a star basketball player, and I knew I had to make the team if my dad was to be proud of me. I had to make the team so I could prove to myself and everyone else that I actually had value.

After tryouts and before the announcement of who made the team, the coaches sent all the players out of the gym and into the cafeteria. Our stage sat at the front end of the cafeteria, which was where I nervously awaited the coaches' return. As the head coach began to read the names of the players who made the team, I could barely contain my emotions. I knew the team was going to consist of twelve or fewer players, and there were nearly forty kids trying out. He began to read the names. One by one, he called the names as I counted. Ninth: not me. Tenth: not me. Eleventh: not me. Twelfth: Dan Gomer. As he read off my name, I was so excited I shouted out, "Yes!"

Every kid in the room turned around and started laughing. I even remember a few kids in front of me saying, "What an idiot." I immediately regretted my outburst.

As the main group began to break up, a small group of players who also made the team decided to make sure I understood my place in the hierarchy. They came up to me and said things like, "You're so lucky that they called your name," "You shouldn't have even made the team," "So-and-so is way better than you," "That was so funny how you yelled when you made the team." Even in my moment of triumph, I was quickly reminded of my place. Although I made the team, I still didn't belong there.

As eighth grade continued, my anger issues and feelings of insecurity, and my frustrations of never fitting in, grew. The frustration of just wanting to be a fun-loving kid who didn't care about clothes and pop culture grew. I was increasingly angry. I was lonely. I was confused. I was sad. No one at school or at home truly understood who I was and, as far as I was concerned, no one had any faith that I had the ability to do anything well.

Although I had strong feelings of insecurity, I was never one to sit back and fade into the background. I had too much to offer this world, and I knew it. This is where a lot of my frustration originated. There was a disconnect between who I *knew* myself to be versus who I *believed* myself to be. I knew I had much to offer, but I believed I had no real value. Eventually, my anger and frustration led to the creation of a thick shell that no one could ever penetrate. "Bring it, bitch!" might as well have been my mantra. Given my big stature, a big personality, and a known unwillingness to back down, it became socially acceptable and even part of the fun for my peers to mess with me. On a daily basis, they would "poke" me to get a rise, and I was always willing to oblige. Of course, this led to continued fighting, feelings of inadequacy and frustration, and a deepening depression.

The fights became more violent and more publicized. One fight in particular drew a great deal of attention. Once everyone caught wind of the animosity, they couldn't help but make sure we settled it after school. One day, we were waiting for the bus to arrive. About fifty kids surrounded this kid and I, and they egged us into a fight. I could feel the anger well up, and I tried to unleash all of it at one time on this one person. Just then, the principal stepped into the circle. He grabbed me by the neck and pulled us both out of the circle. The fight was over, my opponent was crying, and I felt proud that I had settled this. My knuckles were bleeding, and my ego was full. My heart, on the other hand, was not.

As I got older, I started having nightmares about seriously hurting others. I had so much rage in my heart—so much pain. Around the time I entered high school and after years of fighting, anger, and aggression, I finally decided I was done defending myself with force.

Nonetheless, during my eighth-grade year, I felt hopeless. I didn't get it. Why didn't I fit in? I was nice; I genuinely cared for others; I was giving. There had to be something fundamentally wrong with me. I began to believe I was a bad person who didn't deserve to win, didn't have the ability to succeed, didn't fit in, and had no support from anyone. I was alone and lost, and I deserved what was dished out.

Eventually, these daily routines of self-loathing led to thoughts of suicide. When I was thirteen, I vividly remember sitting in my dad's basement with a bottle of gun cleaner. I had no idea what it would do to me when I drank it, but I just wanted the pain to end. I was convinced that no one loved me, and that the world wouldn't even miss me. Why was I here? I was tired of fighting, and I was tired of trying. Nothing I tried ever worked. I was a loser. I was a bad person who would never succeed or fit in. I was done. I opened the cap. As tears streamed down my face, I put the bottle to my lips. I sat there for what seemed like an eternity, trying to figure out what I should do. After some time, I pulled the bottle from my lips and sobbed uncontrollably in a dark basement room all by myself until I finally fell asleep. Thankfully, I wasn't quite there yet. I wasn't able to go through with it.

As I entered high school, I felt unsupported by coaches, parents, and peers. I quit fighting physically, but the fight inside myself raged on. I was dying inside. I played basketball and football, but I didn't fit in with my peers there. I didn't play in band, sing in choir, or act in drama. I had a few acquaintances, but no strong relationships. I saw that everyone else had a clique. High school was a time for my shadows to grow into deep-rooted beliefs about myself. The shadows were now integrating into my being, and the feelings of inadequacy and loneliness began to run my life.

After a tough breakup late in my junior year, I began to contemplate who I wanted to be. In retrospect, the big emotional swing I experienced after the breakup was the catalyst for many of the changes I started to make in my life. I quit going to my usual church. I quit playing football. I did go out for basketball, but for the first time, in my senior year, I did not make the team. After tryouts, I asked the coach why, and his response was that I was lacking the heart this year. I essentially shrugged my shoulders and said "Whatever." I didn't want to play with my would-be teammates anyway. I felt abandoned by all, and I could care less about any of them. So, in my senior year, I played no sports and decided to go outside of my school to meet new people.

Instead of playing for my school, I joined a church basketball team, where I saw more success and I met new people, some of whom I am still friends with today. I was in the very early stages of walking my own path and removing myself from negative environments. Looking back, I now realize that this was another pivotal moment in my life. I was finally learning how to step into my true being and my true power. When we choose to align with who we really are, we are gifted with moments of clarity, and our power springs forth. Don't get me wrong; I still had/have a long way to go. But in the end, this struggle was the birthplace of a new me.

In college, I finally had an opportunity to leave pieces of "old Dan" behind and create a whole new persona. Of course, as much as we would like to think we can leave our past behind, no one can create a new persona without some of the same programs running in the background. While this "new Dan" was able to make people laugh, build strong friendships, and fit in, there were also times when my old programs popped up to say hello. I was not aware enough at the time to know what was going on, but although I was making great strides forward, those shadows from my past were still running the show.

Over time, I began to learn that if I used sarcasm and humor, I could make people laugh and like me. So I began to channel my anger and frustration into sarcasm, joking, goofy behavior, self-deprecation, and partying. I built some strong relationships that I still have today and felt like I belonged. Given that, I still had a great deal of anger, and I was still unhappy. I was simply getting better at hiding and denying it. I became astute at judging others, and I regularly pointed out how other people were doing things the wrong way. Being a person who was constantly judged, the irony is not lost on me. At times I was so happy and grateful, and the next moment I experienced feelings of depression and self-loathing. I was very confused, but I was thinking and I was questioning. I was becoming more aware.

THE NEXT CHAPTER

I graduated college when I was twenty-three, got my first teaching job at twenty-four, married at twenty-five, and began coaching high school basketball at age twenty-six. During these years, I spent most of my free time hanging out with friends, going to the bar, partying, and talking with people about life. I was very curious at this time, but I didn't have the awareness necessary to make powerful shifts in my life. In essence, I didn't know what I didn't know, but I was moving in the right direction.

I was able to build strong relationships and things seemed good on the outside, but inside, I often felt like a fraud. I felt like I was putting on a show in an effort to fit in. It was only a matter of time before everyone realized that I was just the weird kid again.

In many ways, I was destroying myself from the inside out. I created stories about myself that were based on events that happened ten or fifteen years ago, and then I allowed those stories to run my life. I went out into the world looking for ways to prove myself right. I would find proof everywhere that I wasn't good enough. Anytime something would shine light on one of my inadequacies, I would fixate on the issue, lash out at others, or tear myself down. It was a self-fulfilling prophecy.

On the flip side, when events would show up that would prove me wrong, e.g., I would succeed or do something amazing, I would downplay it and remind myself of my place in this world. *Careful, Dan, don't get cocky,* or *Remember, Dan, success is fleeting. Stay grounded.* It's hard to dig yourself out of a rut, when you keep digging under your own feet.

The irony is that, although I thought I had everyone believing that I was strong, confident, successful, and happy, I really wasn't fooling anyone. We all think we are so clever when we wear our masks. We think we have everyone fooled. But we don't! Have you ever looked at someone else and said, "Man, if that person would just do this and that, then they would be doing great. It's so easy, why don't they see it?" Well, here's the kicker: people say that same stuff about all of us. We just can't hear it. We can't hear it because we are too busy finding ways to prove ourselves right about the things we already know to be true. We don't need feedback from anyone, because we are all pros at hearing what confirms our beliefs and dismissing ideas that hurt our ego or go against what we think we know.

After a handful of years as a teacher and coach, I was forced to admit to myself that teaching was not the calling I had once thought it to be. So, I began to devise my exit strategy.

Eventually, I decided that flipping houses was the way to go. I loved real estate, and I knew it would provide fantastic opportunities. I also get to be my own boss! I just needed money, and a mentor.

The mentor was easy. One of my brother's best friends was a realtor, and he knew the business well. He showed me the ropes and became instrumental to my initial success.

Next, I needed money, and a lot of it. I really didn't have a whole lot of options, so I went to my in-laws and asked for a substantial loan. After some discussion, they agreed to give me the money. Now I was making progress. I had a plan, a mentor, and some money.

Here's where the story gets interesting. I made the decision to start a new career from scratch, take a loan from my in-laws, and take a job with no guaranteed income, all while my wife was about three months pregnant with our first child. In retrospect, I have only one thought: *What the hell was I thinking?* I knew the stakes were high, but I had no idea what was coming over the next few years. This decision stretched me so far out of my comfort zone that it nearly broke me, and perhaps that is exactly what I needed.

My first fix-n-flip project was one of the hardest things I

have ever done. This was the first time in my life that I literally worked myself to complete exhaustion. I worked twelve- to fifteen-hour days, seven days a week, for about forty-five days. These were days of intense physical labor, coming home to help with our colicky six-month-old son, combined with the stress of worrying about the project budget, looking for my next project, and managing everything. To say the least, this first project was all-encompassing. A few days before the house was to hit the market, I had to pull a couple all-nighters. I was so tired that the day before the listing went live, I threw up in the bathroom and then fell asleep on a couch that had been placed there by the stagers. I had nothing left in my tank, and I can honestly say that I left it all out on the field during this time.

After forty-five days of working myself to the bone, missing tons of time with my son, and driving myself into the ground, I was finally ready to list. We sold the house fairly quickly, and at close I was able to collect my check, which showed a whopping profit of $5,000.

I remember looking back and saying, "What the hell!" I couldn't believe I did all that for a measly $5,000. Even writing this and thinking back to that time, I begin to get stressed, tired, and a little nauseated. In the end, however, I recognized that this was my first project. So I chalked this one up to a learning experience, and I told myself that the next one would be better. I realized that if I was to succeed at this, I needed to learn how to lead others and learn how to run a business. Little did I know where this realization would take me.

If I was going to be a leader, I needed to learn, so I started reading. The first book I read was *How to Win Friends and Influence People*. It is an amazing book that teaches how to connect with people in a meaningful way and how to work with people so they are on board with a common goal. Next up, *Think and Grow Rich*. I read a book every two weeks or so, and I was loving it. I was shocked at how little I knew about leadership and business. If only I had known this when I was teaching and coaching. What a difference that would have made!

Within the first year and half after leaving teaching, I had completed about four projects, obtained my real estate license, worked a mentorship with the owner of my brokerage, and had a busted partnership with another investor. I was finally becoming an experienced real estate investor. Right around this time, I met my new business partner and one of my best friends. Over the next few years, we ended up partnering on a number of projects. Needless to say, it was a wild ride, full of ups and downs.

My partner, Troy, was the first person to really introduce me to the world of personal developmental books and training. The first book he recommended was *Wishes Fulfilled* by Wayne Dyer. That book changed my life. Then I read *The Shadow Effect* by Deepak Chopra, Marianne Williamson, and Debbie Ford. This book opened my eyes to the idea that I had all these programs running in the background, of which I was completely unaware.

After reading *The Shadow Effect*, I began to recognize some of my shadows. I realized that I had massive amounts of pent-up anger toward my father and my high school basketball coach. In retrospect, these two people were not the actual source of all my problems, but the stories I had created around my experiences with them were the source of much of my anger.

I was nearing my mid-thirties, I was still flipping houses, and I was working through some of my more obvious demons with a shadow coach. Although I still looked happy on the outside and although I was starting to see the light, my internal self-deprecation continued.

Over the three-year period when I was flipping houses, I completed about a dozen projects and, in the end, I made a grand total of nothing. In fact, I lost *a lot* of money. Between growing a business, living expenses, and a couple bad deals, I was in a $180,000 hole. I didn't know how I was going to get out.

While working on my last few projects, it became clear to me that the real estate market was changing, and flipping homes didn't make much sense anymore. So I decided to leverage the experience I had gained while flipping, and use that to help other people buy and sell homes. It turned out to be a really good fit for me. I love building relationships, I love building a business, and I started to see some success.

However, the success felt like it came so … very … slowly— painfully slow. What I didn't realize at the time was that creating a brand new business takes time. I truly thought that I would just let everyone know I had some great real world real estate experience (which is very true), and everyone would hire me, and off we would go. Unfortunately, that's not the way it went down.

It makes sense to stop here and look at the facts versus the story. I didn't realize this until much later, but what was happening was that I had a huge inferiority complex that stemmed from my days on the elementary school playground. If I failed, they were all right and it was true: I'm a loser! If I succeeded, then they were full of shit: I'm a winner! I had built a very elaborate web of deception that allowed me to lie to myself about why I wanted to succeed. I thought I wanted security, time, money, retirement, and so on. In reality, I just wanted to succeed to prove all those "a-holes" wrong. Once and for all, I would prove to them that I was a winner! Suck it! I had disguised this disowned quality so well that I didn't figure out this piece of the puzzle until years after I made the transition from a real estate investor into a full time realtor.

Since things were not going as well as I wanted, and since I hadn't yet developed a strong awareness about what was really going on within myself, there was only one story I could tell myself: I was a loser. The walls began to close in. I had massive debt that I couldn't repay, two young children, and a lot of responsibility. People were depending on me. Winter was setting in, and I knew the slow season was just around the corner. I had no deals on the horizon. I had only a few months' worth of income saved up, Christmas was a few weeks away, and I had no idea where I was going to get my next paycheck. This was it. I failed. *It's over. They were right and you're a loser, Dan!* I had let down my partner; I had let down my in-laws; I had let down my wife; I had let down my kids; I had let down everyone. It was all my fault. I finally found the confirmation for what I already believed about myself: I was never going to succeed.

I'm a big fat failure.

Have you ever felt that way? It's like a bullshit avalanche. Your brain keeps talking in circles, and you just reiterate all the ways you are terrible, over and over again. It's a rough place to be.

At thirty-five, with a nice house, a wife, and two kids, my thoughts of suicide had come full circle. I felt just like I did when I was sitting in my dad's basement. With people all around me, I felt so alone. I felt so abandoned and so ashamed.

In my haze, I began to think, *Maybe I should just end it here. I am worthless anyway, and it would be so much easier.* I know, it's messed up, but that's the truth. Some of you know exactly what I am talking about. Even if you don't contemplate suicide, you can still be in this same headspace. We have all been in a hopeless place where it seems like things can't get worse.

Granted, the choice to end it all *would* be easier. But for whom? That's right—easier for me. Me, me, me, me, me. At this time, I was only thinking about me. And many times, that is what happens in those moments of despair. Our world gets really small.

Only by the grace of God do I have the ability to write this story today. I remember sitting on my bed, in the middle of the day, with no one around, and all these thoughts running through my mind—completely dejected.

Then, a miracle happened. Completely out of the blue, I had a moment of clarity. I don't know where it came from, but it happened in an instant, and it was profound and powerful. Call it God, the universe, or whatever, but for a brief moment, I was snapped out of my trance. I became aware that I had a choice. That's all it took. I thought to myself, *What the hell are you doing, man? Time to choose. End it now, or figure this out. What are you going to do?*

This one realization allowed me to snap out of my trance. My world began to expand. I thought about my wife and kids, and I recognized that I had just been given a gift. I had been given the gift of looking over the edge and saying, "Not today." I had too much to offer this world to throw it all away over some story. It happened that fast. From total despair to an unshakable realization that I have so much to live for. Right then and there, I dedicated myself to never going back to that place.

By going to the brink and then taking a step back, I was able to make one of the most steadfast commitments in my life, and it was one of the most powerful events I have ever experienced.

THE POWER OF OUR STORIES

This is a perfect example of why it is so important to understand our stories. I truly believe that through the work I had done up to this point, I had a spark of intuition that shined through in my greatest moment of struggle. I was reminded that I was living in a story, and that I have the power to change this story anytime I want.

I will never go back to that place again. I was given a second chance, and I realized that day that I am going to find my greatness. That is what I do every day now. Greatness is not perfection, success, adoration, being the best dad, or any of those things. Greatness is looking within every day and simply trying to be the best version of myself—being a better person today than I was yesterday.

This was where my practice of self-reflection, working with coaches, meditation, yoga, and personal growth began. This moment of great pain turned into my greatest asset. Times were still tough after that moment. The facts didn't change. But my story did! I was going to figure it out, and I did.

Today, I have a clear vision about who I want to be and how I want to show up in the world. I know how I want to change the world, and I am confident in my abilities. I know the value that I bring to the world, and I know I have light to give. I recognize that I have shortcomings and I know I have work to do, but I do my best to embrace and love every part of myself as I do this work. I am changing the world with intention, and it all began with an awareness and a curiosity to understand my life and my story.

At the end of the day, it doesn't matter what's actually happening in our lives. What matters is the *story* we tell ourselves about who we are. What might be a big deal to you could be a small deal to me and vice versa. The question I challenge you to ask yourself is this: What is the story you are telling yourself?

There are no peaks without the valleys. That is what this book is all about. It's about becoming aware so we can overcome the odds and find new leases on life. It's about working on ourselves, stepping into our power, and then sharing with others about how to make their life better. It's about realizing how similar we all are. It's about creating a better world and a better mental landscape for us all.

**It's about struggle, and it's about the
growth that always follows.**

YOUR STORY

Although you may be able to pull some insight about your own life by listening to my story, at the end of the day, your story is where the answers lie for you. Have you ever considered writing out your story? Perhaps you should. It has been very therapeutic for me to reflect on and write my story. I would recommend you do the same. Who knows what you will learn about yourself? After all, you have to know your story if you ever hope to change your world from within.

I bring before you a challenge and an opportunity to physically write out your story. Putting your life experiences down on paper allows you to learn about the most important person in your life: *you*! Remember, the more you know about you, the easier it is to love yourself. The more you love yourself, the more you love life. The more you love life, the more the world opens up. When the world opens up, you have complete control of your destiny. It starts here!

Here are a few tips that I used when writing my story that seemed to really help.

First, I like to meditate and get my mind still before I write. I'll talk about meditation in a later chapter, but for now I will just say that meditation can be a powerful tool that may help you dig deeper within yourself.

Second, just write a sentence. It doesn't matter what the

sentence says, but just get something down. Your writing may follow that first sentence or take off on a completely different tangent. It doesn't matter. What matters is that you get the first sentence written. That will open the floodgates and allow the flow of ideas. Once the ideas begin to flow, keep going. Write ideas down as they pop into your head for later reference. Who cares if it makes sense at first? You can go back later and re-organize it. No rules here; you can clean it up later. For right now, just write it down and feel it. You will be amazed what comes out of you. You are a powerful person with a powerful story to share. Share it all. Don't hold yourself back. Let it flow, and write it all down.

Third, pretend you are writing a fictional story about someone else. Even though the character may be based on your life, thinking about your experiences in the third person will allow you to tell the story from a new perspective. It will allow you to see other facts that may get lost when you are trapped in the first person.

Fourth, feel the emotions that you felt at the time. Experience your entire life with complete compassion and unrestrained emotion. Tap into your main character's journey, just like you would if you were reading a fictional story. Take the time and energy to cry with your character when they are treated unfairly. Feel the anger when someone takes advantage of your character. Laugh when your character does something stupid or embarrassing. Don't hold back. Sure, you may look like an idiot if someone walked in on you while you are uncontrollably sobbing in front of a computer typing out some ridiculous story from when you were eight, but that's the point! Writing your story and feeling it fully allows you to have compassion for yourself.

This process also allows you to vent and let out pent-up emotions that you haven't let yourself feel since you were eight. That's a long time to keep silly emotions pent up, and it takes unimaginable energy to hold on to those emotions. Sometimes you may see yourself crying over something that seems so silly, but here's the reality: You have been holding onto that stupid story for twenty, thirty, forty, or even fifty or more years. Let it out. Feel your pain, feel your joy, feel your stress, and experience your successes and your failures. Experience your life through the eyes of a fictional character, and fully experience who you are and where you come from. This is your opportunity to see yourself for who you are: a flawed person who is perfect in the eyes of the universe. Here is your opportunity to see yourself as a human. Remember that you are full of all of it.

As you write and relive your story, feel compassion, just as you would if it actually were a fictional character. This is your opportunity to stop putting the events in your life into the context of your story. Compassion for yourself is key. Many times during this process, strong emotions will come up. It is imperative that you are compassionate toward yourself. If you get wrapped up in *your* story rather than a *fictional* story, then you will have a tendency to lose awareness, and that can derail the process. This is a practice in self-exploration, not a practice of finding proof of self-defeating thoughts about yourself. You have been doing the latter for your whole life. How has that been working out? Now it's time to look at your life in a different light. See yourself as a child who has been wounded. See yourself as a person with desires and ambition. See yourself as a person who deserves to succeed.

Fifth, write it as if it is a book that will be published, and everyone will read it. This doesn't mean that you actually have to share it with anyone, and it doesn't have to have perfect grammar, sentence structure, and flow. All it means is that it is important to treat this exercise with respect. Write this story to the best of your ability. Put time and effort into your creation. Find the details. There were many details that I left out, but I didn't want my story to drag on while you were reading it, so my story is purposely abridged in this publication only. When you write your story, write your story fully. Add all details you want. The idea here is that you write a story that encompasses your life. It is hard to do that if you are writing a quick synopsis. After all, this is your life story.

Finally, enjoy the experience. Although it may be challenging, this should be fun. You finally get the opportunity to tell your story to the world, and you finally have the opportunity to understand yourself better. For me, just getting my story down on paper and feeling it fully was one of the most therapeutic experiences of my life. Not only that, but it was a lot of fun. Memories I hadn't thought about for years came flooding back, and I was able to relive my life through the eyes of a stranger. Full of compassion and love, I was able to reunite with that little boy inside of myself and become whole again. My challenge to you: Just do it!

PART II

ROADBLOCKS

*"We can't fight darkness with darkness.
We have to find compassion, and embrace the
darkness inside of us in order to understand
it and, ultimately, to transcend it."*

—Debbie Ford

THROUGH DENIAL AND DISTRACTION, we fail to look at ourselves with honesty and love. We deny pieces of ourselves that we wish didn't exist, and we distract ourselves from accepting these "bad" qualities through TV, drama, anger, alcohol, adrenaline rushes, gaming, judgment, food, excuses, and blame. Our vices allow us to continually deny our true self, which in turn creates our shadow self. Because we are ultimately unaware of our shadows and programs, our subconscious and ego run our lives and we lose the power of choice.

As our ego grows, we subconsciously spend our days vigorously defending it in an effort to be right. Many times this mission to be right comes at the cost of our own happiness and contentment. We could care less about being happy, as long as we are right! As our discontent grows, we look outward for ways to protect our fragile ego, grasping at straws as we seek to blame someone or something other than ourselves for our life circumstances. It must be "them." However, the more we look outward, the more we lose alignment within ourselves. This is when fear brews within us—fear that we may be the problem *and* the solution to our own life circumstances.

As the fear arises, we are given a choice. Oftentimes, rather than taking 100 percent responsibility for our life and looking inward to find alignment, we once again distract ourselves and blame others. Ultimately, this pattern creates more fear and discontent, which then leads to anger, frustration, and pain. The cycle repeats itself until the end of our days.

Whew, there is a lot to unpack there! As we begin, please remember that through awareness, honesty, and compassion, we all have the ability to shift our life at any time.

In the next five chapters we will start to get real. We will begin to look at all the things that hold us back. I call these roadblocks. Many of the roadblocks we will cover stem from a perception of lack, which can make the topics a bit heavy, so stick with me. I promise we will lighten things back up again in later chapters.

It can be hard to look inward and admit that we actually are wrong sometimes. It can also be hard to admit that we are, in fact, the architects of every aspect of how we show up in the world and how we feel about ourselves. In other words, we are the architects of every facet of our lives. It can be a challenge to truly take responsibility and begin the work toward our most powerful self. I ask that as you read the coming chapters, you do two things. First, reflect upon your life with brutal honesty. Use this as an opportunity to look inward and discover your role and your responsibility for the creation of your life.

Second, please be kind to yourself. We have all done things we are not proud of, we have all had horrible things happen to us, and we all struggle. We all screw up and we can all be better. This goes for you, too. Show compassion for yourself as you discover things that have been holding you back, and know that awareness of these pieces is the beginning of a whole new *you*.

CHAPTER 3

LACK OF SELF-REFLECTION

"Let go of who you think you are supposed to be and embrace who you are."

—Brene Brown

THIS IS WHERE THE PROCESS of changing our life begins. There is one thing that holds us all back from taking the first step toward a fulfilled life: ourselves. Our reluctance to endure the necessary struggle of self-reflection and reframing of our mind is the root of the status quo. Self-reflection is where the journey toward changing the world begins and in some form, all other parts of the coming chapters flow back to this concept. If we want to change the world with intention, we must look within, learn, implement, and repeat. This will create a powerful pattern that allows us to become more aware, which, in turn, gives us the power of choice. And when we get to choose, we get to become everything we always desired to be.

If I told you I am going to break both of your legs at the knee without anesthesia, but once you heal, you will be able to run faster and jump higher than any human who ever lived, would you let me do it? I know this is a dramatic question, but what it really represents is an opportunity to experience pain for an ultimate greater growth.

What I am trying to say is that when we start down the path of self-awareness and personal development, this is essentially what we do to our soul. We bring our ego to its knees and make it question whether it is actually right. We make our ego relent to reality. The ego doesn't like this at all. The ego is here to protect our righteousness. I wholeheartedly believe this is why so few people are willing to do the work it takes to create lasting change. It's easier to keep the knees the way they are, so to speak, even if the knees we are protecting are fragile and full of pain.

On the flip side, those who are willing to break the knees of their ego, through honest self-reflection and enduring the struggle, gain the benefits of choice, power, freedom, and contentment. So, I ask again. If I told you I am going to break your ego and bring your spirit to its knees, without anesthesia, but once you heal, you will be able to enjoy every moment, create lasting change in your life and the lives of those around you, and see the world in a whole new light, would you let me do it?

OUR SHADOW SELF

One of the beautiful things about self-reflection is that it allows us to discover pieces of ourselves that we never even knew existed. These unconscious drivers of our life are called shadows. Our shadows are programs that control our day-to-day actions. Shadows usually stem from a combination of disowned aspects of ourselves and the masks that we use to cover up those disowned qualities. Over time, these shadow beliefs and masks become so deeply rooted that they run our lives without us even knowing it. I call this autopilot.

Simply put, we often carry trauma from events that happened to us before the age of ten. Those are the years that we develop our stories and fill our "blank slate of a mind" with the reality of our world and our place in it. These experiences become engrained in our psyche, and this worldview creates our guiding principles for the rest of our life. Unless we do something about it.

The ironic part of all of this is that when we were this young, we usually lacked the wisdom to truly understand the circumstances of what was happening. Regardless, our young brains needed to create a worldview. So it would make sense that a child experiences an event, creates a story (accurate or not) about the event, and then ultimately makes a judgment about the world or themselves based on that story. This interpretation is created without a lot of filters or wisdom, so you can see how this may create problems later on. There are many benefits to being youthful, but unfortunately, wisdom comes only with age and experience.

Susan Tzankow, one of the most influential coaches in my life, likens a shadow story to this. Let's say it's your first day of kindergarten. Your mom drops you off at school and gives you a big hug and kiss. As she leaves, she tells you that she will be here at three o'clock sharp to pick you up and hear all about your day. As the school day comes to an end, your mother is nowhere to be found. Three o'clock comes and goes. Three-thirty comes and goes. Finally, at four, your mom shows up. You have now had sixty minutes to sit and think and create stories about what this event means. Additionally, you don't have the life experience yet to consider outside circumstances that could have affected her tardiness. In this scenario, there is no telling what our story might look like, and there is no telling how long we might hold onto the beliefs created during this short sixty-minute life experience.

Here's the reality. Your mom simply got a flat tire on the way to school and had to call AAA to come replace it. She left her cell phone on the counter and didn't have a way to call the school. She meant no harm and felt absolutely horrible.

The unfortunate reality is that the damage is already done. There is nothing she can say that can change your new story. A fear of being left behind was created, which led to a shadow creation that will now run in the background of your life for years to come. You may become a people pleaser, because then people won't leave. You may become a loner, because people can't leave if no one is there. You may become a class clown, because people like to hang out with funny kids.

In this scenario, you have created a belief, your ego latches onto that belief, and then your ego goes on the lookout for proof of what you already know to be "true." Over time, your ego runs with this tiny seed and finds evidence everywhere that proves you have been left behind. Now that your ego has found evidence all over the place, you can sink into an engrained life story, which then self-propagates. You get the idea. How this shadow manifests is unique to each individual, but the key point is that this shadow *will* show up, and as you grow older, the shadow strengthens and becomes increasingly rooted in our psyche if we don't become aware of it. Until we recognize, accept, love, and reintegrate these shadows, they will run in the background of our life, whether we like it or not.

We all do this all the time. Even today. The magic of growth begins when we begin to open up to the idea that maybe the stories we have told ourselves are full of inaccuracies and harsh self-criticism. Maybe those events were actually more about someone else and less about us.

OUR MASKS

Think about a train. On this train, you have all sorts of passengers. The train represents our whole being, and all the passengers represent pieces of ourselves, or our *personas*. Any one persona has the capability to act as a great asset or to cause great destruction.

There is a reason why each of these passengers are on the train to begin with. Every passenger has earned his or her ticket through the service and value they gave at some point in our life. This train is a culmination of our life lessons and wisdom, fears, shadows, tendencies, and strengths.

As one might imagine, we tend to play favorites with our passengers. We find pieces of our-selves that we think look good or appealing to the world, and we ask them to sit in the front of the train. We think that by bringing certain traits to the forefront, no one will ever see who is sitting in the back. Another name for this would be "putting on a mask."

Some masks are very intricate and clever. Some masks are ugly and easy to see through, but the fact remains, we all wear masks to try to conceal the ugly reality that is our train. And even though we think our masks are super clever, I can tell you now, they might as well be made out of Saran Wrap because the rest of the world can usually see right through them.

We may put on a mask of perfection to hide feelings of inferiority, incompetence, or shame. We may put on a mask of happiness to hide pain, uneasiness, or worry. We may put on a mask of success to hide feelings of failure, unworthiness, or poverty. We put on the mask of humor to hide feelings of self-loathing, confusion, or depression. We may put on the mask of motivation to simply hide feelings. Notice that all these masks are essentially overcompensations for pieces of ourselves that we have disowned. At some point, we felt badly about ourselves for x, y, and z, so now we will do the exact opposite to prove to ourselves and to the world that x, y, and z are not who we truly are. Welcome, shadow!

As we get older and gain wisdom, our train fills with more passengers. Eventually, we realize that some passengers serve us well and get us what we want. Others served us well in the past, but now they seem to just get us in trouble. Naturally, our first inclination is to attempt to hide, shame, and stuff "bad" personas in the back of the train. With little to no gratitude for their past service, we tell those pieces of ourselves that they are no longer needed and they should sit in the back and shut it. These "bad" aspects, which once acted as our savior and only saving grace, now reside, shamed, in the back of the train. They long to once again serve a purpose, to once again belong, and to once again be relevant. They're like a child waiting for the right moment to shine, in an effort to remind us of how important they are. Even though we believe personas may not serve us like they once did, the fact remains that they are part of who we are and they need to be acknowledged.

As much as you want them to just go away, those fiery disowned personas are here to stay. And they make a point to imprint ugly little reminders about their existence all over your beautifully designed mask. Unfortunately, when we are unaware of our disowned qualities, they tend to remind us of their existence at the most inopportune times. As soon as we let down our guard, they rear their ugly heads and come out in ways we are not proud of. Like that time you got wasted at the Christmas party and decided it was the perfect moment to let your boss know what you *really* thought about his new policy for internet use in the office. In reality, our disowned qualities actually own us. We wonder why we continue these patterns of self-destruction. It's just our shadows, sticking some gum under the seat and throwing their little heads out the train window and yelling, "Hello!"

When "bad" personas rear their ugly heads and come out sideways, we reprimand ourselves and say, "Why do I keep doing that? I'm better than that. I have to stop doing that." We leverage shame, anger, and sheer will as tools to cover up unwanted passengers while we stuff them further back in the train. Of course, as I mentioned before, those personas are still on the train, and I promise, they will find creative new ways to mess with our mojo. We begin the same cycle again. Clean up the mess, clean off our mask and pretend things will be different next time. I'm getting exhausted by just writing about it.

Eventually we become so good at establishing our shadow self, that we don't even think about it anymore. We simply live each day and do ... you know, stuff and junk. All the while, we're relying on our shadows to mindlessly conduct our train. We live day to day on autopilot. We grind it out and prove to the world who we "really" are: a perfect being with the most beautiful mask, ever! Then we do it again tomorrow.

AWARENESS

Without awareness of every passenger on our train, good or bad, we lose the option of choice. If we become preoccupied with designing our intricate masks while simultaneously disowning qualities we deem to be unworthy, we lose the ability to govern any one aspect of ourselves with intention. Essentially, we lose control of who is conducting our train. All of this is subconscious, of course, but essentially, this is what many of us do every day. We unwittingly lose control of our freedom to choose, and then, out of a sense of ease, we simply settle.

As we strive for perfection, happiness, or success, we simultaneously pretend that anything counter to those desires is nonexistent within us. This internal struggle is a daily practice until it becomes so routine we just accept it as part of life. It's easier to cover up and pretend, rather than revealing to ourselves who we truly are. Then we wonder why we aren't happy, why we aren't content, and why we aren't as successful as we want. Even when we upgrade the house, the job, the vacations, the popularity, the car, the marriage, and so on, we still feel unfulfilled.

All those items I just mentioned are great in the short term, and they can be invigorating. But we all know how fleeting these happy emotions can be when they are linked to short-term gains. Upgrading our most basic needs in lieu of doing real work on our psyche is equivalent to putting a Band-Aid on a bullet wound. It appears to be better than nothing, but ultimately, it is an exercise in futility.

"OK, slow your roll! Are you suggesting that we throw off our masks and express our rawest qualities with complete disregard of the world around us?"

Well, unless you want to look like the crazy person on the side of the road shouting about the voices in your head, then no, I don't think you should do that. I *am* saying that when we recognize that these "bad" pieces of our psyche *are* one of our personas and then give them gratitude for their service, they can serve us when needed and they will sit quietly in the back of the train when they are not. We gain the power of choice through awareness and acceptance of every piece of ourselves, which ultimately allows us to tap into our unimaginable power.

Through awareness, every persona can be used as a tool at the appropriate time. Imagine trying to fix a car. A wrench will serve you well if you want to change your brakes, but it probably won't be needed if you are changing the windshield. Unless you know what tools you have at your disposal, confusion will set in and you won't get much done. If we know what tools we have at our disposal, we can use them when needed and we can leave them in the toolbox when not.

SHADOW STORY

I believe our stories are powerful, so with that in mind, I want to share a quick story about breaking through a shadow belief I held onto for more than thirty years. Although I have been working on myself for a long time, I was completely oblivious to the root cause of this shadow until recently. It's truly amazing how sneaky these little guys can be. Hence, my dedication to this work. As I learn more about my programs and myself, I get to lead the life I truly want and get to change the world with intention.

On a side note, this is why counseling and coaching are so important. Other people are typically very good (and willing) to point out what *our* problems are.

When I was in third grade, there was a kid in my class who, in retrospect, had some anger issues. Who knows what his upbringing was like, and who knows what his home life was like? All I knew was that, for whatever reason, he picked me as a target to bully. He was able to get other kids on his team, and they began to bully me as well. I had no idea why they singled me out. Eventually, the bullying came to a head and being a kid in the mid-eighties, "zero tolerance" wasn't really a thing yet. So I had to settle this on my own.

I didn't know it at the time, but the pain of getting picked on eventually created a few deep-rooted fears. One, the fear of not fitting in; two, the fear of being inferior; and three, the fear of being in danger. Over time, those fears gave way to a mask decorated with self-reliance, toughness, and anger. One day, I decided I wasn't going to take it anymore—the time had come for action. So, I did what I knew how to do, and I attacked him, ferociously. The fight was after school and near the parking lot, so the next thing I remember was his mom digging her giant fake fingernails into the back of my neck as she ripped me off of this kid.

The fight itself is irrelevant, but there is some powerful irony here. Through this entire experience, I had felt inferior, so rather than admitting that I felt inferior, I engrained a long-standing shadow within my psyche that "proved" to the world that I was not.

As I talked about in "My Story," I used to fight a lot when I was younger. I always assumed I fought because I was strong. I attached a positive belief system to my negative behavior. "I will fight anyone, anytime, because I am strong and no one can push me around." There's some truth to this statement. I was strong and people couldn't push me around without me lashing out, but here is the sneaky part. I was able to be strong only because I was operating from a program, "People don't like me,

I am unworthy and lonely, I don't belong, so I must fight and protect myself at all times. Then they can't hurt me anymore."

For most of my life, I was well-aware of the story about being strong. However, for more than thirty years, I was completely unaware of the program that I felt unworthy. I needed the belief that "I am strong and tough" so I could protect myself from admitting that I actually felt unworthy. Shadow/mask = I am strong and no one will push me around. Disowned qualities = unworthiness, loneliness, and inferiority.

Unbeknownst to my conscious mind, my ego, which is tied to my subconscious belief system, now had no choice but to spend the next thirty years finding proof that I was inferior. On the outside, my conscious mind had to protect my mask by proving to the world that "they" were wrong about me, through a constant battle to succeed. I had to create a mask that proved "they can't push me around" and that I was "more than what anyone gave me credit for." Some might call this spite. For much of my life, I put a majority of my energy into a vain attempt to convince the world that I wasn't what I actually believed myself to be. It's exhausting!

With all of that said, we don't hold onto beliefs like this without an upside. That is why I was able to hold this shadow for so long. My shadow created a very strong will to compete and a drive to succeed at all costs. This drive brought much outward success.

Unfortunately, it also came with a price tag. It cost me joy, contentment, alignment, and wholeness. My story was so engrained that I bought into the idea that my unhealthy competiveness and all-consuming drive to succeed were my biggest assets, when in fact, they were destroying me from the inside out. At some point, I realized that the costs were outweighing the benefits. That moment of realization was when I was able to shift my conscious mind and move toward a new, more powerful version of myself.

BLAME AND FORGIVENESS

If failure to look inward and address our shadow is a roadblock, then what stops us from looking inward? I believe Carl Jung says it well: "Everything that irritates us about others can lead us to an understanding about ourselves." Oftentimes, we leverage our old friend, blame, as a way to circumvent self-reflection. It's my boss's fault. It's my spouse's fault. It's my parent's fault. It's the bully's fault. It's the politician's fault. It's the terrorist's fault. It's the abuser's fault. It's God's fault. Whew!

We have talked about shadow and how that can create an unwillingness or fear of looking inward with honesty. By ignoring our shadow and by allowing our fears to run our lives, we are trapped in a never-ending cycle of blame. This should make perfect sense, right? If we refuse to look inward and admit we are to blame for our own unhappiness and incompleteness, the only other option is to look outward and (ironically) blame others for our own personalized worldview.

We have the power to change our worldview any time. But when we blame others, we lock ourselves into a struggle we can't win, because we never address the *real* root cause of the problems: *us!* We are the problem and the solution. We must stop blaming and be brutally honest with ourselves to discover our own role in our life as it currently stands. We have the power to discover solutions that create abundance in our life, now.

I am not saying that no one has ever done us harm. That is obviously not the case. We didn't have control over those terrible events or people, but we do have control over how we react to those events today. I can tell you with 100 percent certainty that as long as the responsibility is being divvied out to others and we take no responsibility personally, the pain will continue until the end of our days. This is a tough pill to swallow, so let me explain.

I am never going to say that these horrible acts that were committed against you, me, us, are our fault. We often have no control when people do bad things to us, especially when we are young. None of us deserves to have these things happen. My heart goes out to you, if painful memories arise as you read this. These can be terrible, and I wish them on no one. However, there is an inconvenient/hard truth here.

As long as we hold onto the blame, we hide behind a wall that gives undue power to our aggressors and inhibits us from moving beyond those experiences.

In other words, our blame keeps us pinned down and trapped. As long as we hold onto blame, rather than taking responsibility for how we *react,* and as long as we hold onto these events, we are under the control of that person who has wronged us, forever. Once we realize we have a choice, we can begin to move forward toward a better life—a life and mindset we control. A life filled with intention.

Taking responsibility for our role in the reaction to the situation *does not* mean taking responsibility for the role others played in these events. These people did something that will create consequences within their life, and they have responsibility for what they have done. With that said, you have responsibility for how *you* react. The longer you blame, the longer you live in a self-created cage of despair.

Do you want to be right, or do you want to be happy?

Have you ever been with a friend or co-worker who constantly points out how the world has wronged them? This person said this or did that, their boss constantly does this or that, their significant other does this or that, or their child's teacher always mistreats their child at school. On and on and on. The world is mistreating them at every turn, and there is nothing this person can do to fix it. As an outsider, it's usually fairly easy to look at their complaints and recognize that they are simply dodging responsibility by blaming the world at large. It's easy to look at someone else and see this pattern. It is much harder to look at ourselves and recognize our role in our own life. Blame is a scapegoat. Blame is easy. Blame is the key to dodging personal growth and responsibility for our actions.

The conundrum is that we are often right as we place blame elsewhere. We can easily find more than enough evidence to prove our point. This person did something horrible, and they are the source of our unhappiness. We ... are ... right. They messed up. Our friends and family have already validated our stories and our stances. We have proven beyond a shadow of a doubt that we're right. There you go. Point made. Now what?

For starters, we can't change what has happened in the past and we can't go back in time to do it differently. So now what? We have a choice. Do we choose to continue to blame, which obviously has not been working, or do we choose to accept responsibility for our *reaction* to these events as we move forward intentionally and take back control of our life?

I'll ask again, do you want to be right or do you want to be happy? You have been right for years, but are you happy? No? Maybe it's time to try something other than blame. Maybe it's time to take responsibility for how you choose to move forward from this moment. Perhaps it's even time for forgiveness. Oh, boy! I just dropped The F-bomb!

This is where things can really come off the rails. Not only do I have to accept responsibility, but I also have to forgive? That's it! I'm outta here! You're crazy if you think I'm going to forgive my in-laws, my parents, my boss, my friend who cheated with my spouse, my cheating spouse, my co-worker…

I may be crazy, but I am also spot on. Truth doesn't care about your feelings, and the truth is that as long as we withhold forgiveness, we withhold happiness from ourselves.

We forgive others because it releases us from having to hold onto negative energy. Contrary to popular belief, we don't forgive to release *others* from wrongdoing. We forgive to release *ourselves* from continued agony. We forgive for our own well-being, not theirs. Forgiveness is an act of self-love.

This is one of those topics that's so simple, it's complicated. Trust me, there are still people who I am working to forgive. But, the longer I live, the more I understand how blame holds me back and forgiveness creates space for my soul to expand.

I can't help but feel that blame and the lack of forgiveness are some of the most prominent root causes of stagnation. We blame and we hold. Our energy becomes stuck and so does our life. So, with that in mind, let's do a quick exercise and move some stuck energy.

EXERCISE

Take out a sheet of paper or open up an empty document on your computer. You are going to answer a few questions and create a few lists. After each question or direction, stop reading and write as much as you can. List as many people or events as you can for each item, and don't stop until you have everything out on paper. Only then, move onto the next item.

Before you begin, do a simple meditation to help quiet your mind. Relax and close your eyes. Place your hands on your lap with your palms up. In a moment, you are going to take five deep breaths. When you take your in-breaths, you will hold the in-breath for five seconds. As your chest expands, lengthen through your neck, and relax your face and shoulder muscles. After five seconds of holding your in-breath, release your breath with an audible sigh and allow your body to sink into a relaxed posture. Do this five times, making sure to fill your lungs fully, extending your chest, relaxing your face, and letting it go with a loud sigh. Then get quiet and let your breathing take on a life of its own. Let your thoughts drift as you focus your breathing. Just relax. Now, open your eyes and begin.

Start by taking a few minutes to reflect on all the bad stuff that has happened to you in your life. Without judgment, just live in that pain for a moment. Show compassion for the struggles you have endured.

Now, begin answering these two questions. Don't think about it too much. Just write as much or as little as you want.

1. When have you felt wronged? Be raw. Be real! Get after it and blame everyone and everything. Don't hold back. Don't worry about what you are actually writing. Just go. Write. Get it all out.
2. Whom do you tend to blame? Write down as many names as you want.

How did that feel? Hopefully, getting all that out felt great! We're not quite done yet, so stick with the process here.

Come back to your breath and take some time to recognize yourself for persevering through everything you just wrote down. You are strong. If you weren't, you wouldn't be here today.

Now, bring these memories back to the forefront of your mind and reflect on how you reacted to all these moments. Write down how these moments have influenced your decisions throughout your life. How have these moments been running your life for *years*?

Take a few deep breaths and recognize yourself again for doing some very challenging soul-searching.

These events happened for a reason, and they played an important role in your life.

With that in mind, write down how your life could be different if you were to accept these events for what they are and then take responsibility for your choices around them as you move forward. What is possible for you today and tomorrow if you stop blaming, and take responsibility for your life moving forward?

Once again, thank yourself for your dedication to seeing your world in a new light. Working through this simple process has already helped you move forward. You should be proud. Take a few more slow, deep breaths and come back to the present.

TAKING RESPONSIBILITY

This exercise is meant to be therapeutic. It's your chance to get your blame out and build some perspective. Let's be real. We all blame, myself included, so let's accept that and lean into it. It is a natural response of the ego. After all, if I admit that I screwed up, then I have to swallow my pride and my ego has to take a hit. No thanks! It should be no surprise then, that we have a natural tendency to blame others on a daily basis.

By looking at ourselves honestly, we begin to understand our role in creating our own life and our own results. Once we find responsibility for our life, we figure out how to show up in the world with intention. The first step of looking inward begins by recognizing blame patterns and then removing blame from our lives.

Blame is soul-poison disguised as righteousness.

Blame, whether deserved or not, keeps us from tapping into our fullest potential. When we rely on the outside world to make us happy, we are setting ourselves up for failure. Blame kills the opportunity for us to grow and flourish, because it blinds us to the beautiful opportunity of awareness and self-reflection.

When we hold onto the blame, those people who have wronged us in the past continue to own our soul. By pointing the finger outward, we lose the gift of turning inward. As I said before, I am not saying that what these people have done to us is OK. I am not saying that you have to let it go and pretend like it is totally fine. That is disillusionment. That is not healthy either. What I am saying is that blame and lack of personal responsibility keep you from living a life of intention. Once you stop blaming and take an honest look at yourself, you will begin to realize that you have the ultimate role in creating the life you desire.

You get to choose how you move forward from here. With that said, self-reflection is a great place to start. It breeds awareness, and self-reflection is key to overcoming shadows, overcoming blame, and taking responsibility. By taking that finger that has been pointing out at the world and turning it back at yourself, you can finally take responsibility for the fact that you are the creator of your own life. Once you can do that, you will to tap into tremendous power and create the life you truly desire.

CHAPTER 4

LACK OF PURPOSE

"The mystery of human existence lies not in just staying alive, but in finding something to live for."

—Fyodor Dostoyevsky

FINDING OUT WHAT MAKES our engine purr is the first step to changing the world with an intention that cannot be derailed. Through practice and dedication, your what/ why will become your knowing and your driving force. Our "what" can be defined as a purpose. Not a goal, but a purpose. Our purpose is something deeper. It is rooted within our most authentic self. As we align with our purpose, we begin to understand more and more why that purpose fuels us. Once we know what we want and why we want it, all that's left is to avoid distractions as we create the life we have always dreamed of.

PURPOSE

I have a quick question for you. How do you get there? Get where, you ask? Exactly. How do we get "there" when we don't know where there is?

Have you ever heard someone say, "I just want to be happy"? I know I have. Often, there is a lot of irony in that statement, because many times people say they want to be happy, yet they have no idea what happy looks like to them and they don't know why happy is their end game. In other words, they are not clear on where "there" is. It's no surprise then that this conundrum leads to frustration and another common question: "*Why* can't I just be happy?"

The idea of needing to know where you are going may seem obvious and simplistic, but it is one of the most well-known and most neglected principles in creating intentional change. Knowing what you truly want may be a simple idea, but it can sometimes be tough to create clarity around these desires, especially if your desires are big. It takes dedication and a willingness to self-reflect while exploring *the* question: "What do I want out of life and *why* is that important?"

Goals are great, and we will talk about them in the next section, but goals are simply a means to an end. Before we start setting goals, we have to know exactly what it is that we are trying to create.

We can create routine desires like increasing our income or

traveling more, but that's small potatoes. The title of this book says "Let's change the world together!" The desires I am talking about here are much bigger than those tiny objectives. What I am talking about is finding a *purpose*. One that fuels your soul and makes you want to get up in the morning. I'm talking about an idea or a project that inspires you as you change the world.

Discovering a purpose in life is absolutely essential to finding contentment, fulfillment, wholeness, and joy. Don't get me wrong; I am not here to tell anyone what their purpose should be. For one person it may be helping others in their community, and for another it may mean going to Africa to build schools. What I am saying is that no matter our purpose, when we discover the reason for why we have been put here on earth, we find fulfillment.

Once you have an unwavering desire and once you know why that is important to you, your purpose will drive all the other goals and you will see success and growth in just about every facet of your life. I could go on, but I will end this section with a quote attributed to Mark Twain that sums up my message in one sentence: "The two most important days in life are the day you are born and the day you find out why."

GOALS

Let's shift gears for a moment and talk about goal-setting. First of all, there are a lot of great goal-setting books out there. For the purposes of this book, we will simply touch on why goal-setting is so hard and why a lack of goals keeps us from an intentional life.

Setting goals is essential, because if we have no defined goal, we are destined to chase some vague, unattainable, pie in the sky objective. For example, "I want to be happy." What does that mean? By when do you want to be happy? How do you know when you have finally reached the stage of "happy"? Without a real goal, there is no finish line, there is no completion, and there is no defined success. Garbage goals in, garbage results out. Without a goal, we run around in circles our whole life asking the same question, "Why can't I just …?" You can't just … because you have no clear definition about what you want out of life, so creating an intentional life becomes absolutely impossible.

With that said, anyone can write down a bunch of uninspired goals all day long. Setting great, defined, actionable goals is hard. Just like anything, it takes practice, dedication, honesty, contemplation, reflection, commitment, intention, and focus. For many people, this is where the wheels start to come off, because it takes a lot of energy to work in this place of complete focus.

It has taken me years of practice to learn how to develop goals that align with who I am and what I want. In fact, I am (and forever will be) reflecting and updating my goals. I have a desire to create an intentional life; therefore, I have dedicated myself to asking the questions of what do I want and why, over and over and over again.

I am going to hop on the coaching train again. My coaches and counselors have been instrumental in helping me boil down my goals into the essence of what I really desire. If you are serious about leading an intentional life, go find a coach!

Even when working with skilled coaches, the answers to what we want in life are tied up in a complex web and they don't always seem to come as easily as we might hope. This means that, along with working with coaches, it is imperative that we find a daily practice where we get quiet and sit with our thoughts.

"Hold on, Dan, are you saying I am going to have to stop, get quiet, eliminate distractions, and then listen to those crazy voices in my head?"

Yep!

"That sounds terrible. I may just switch to a different book. I hear vampires are super hot right now!"

I hear you, and I know this may sound hard at first. But it's just like anything else. The more you practice, the easier it gets. It all starts with a simple intention: "I am going to discover my mission in life."

I'm laying down a challenge to you. If you want to create change in your life and live with intention, then it's time to accept that it takes a lot of effort. Get comfortable with being uncomfortable. This is why most people simply choose to do it tomorrow.

Let's look at an example: I want a donut, so to get a donut, I have to clearly define the goal. My goal is "Go get a donut, right now." Phase 1 is now complete. So how do I go about getting that delicious, delicious donut?

If I simply say to myself, "I want some junk food," there is a high likelihood that I will sit on the couch and binge watch *Game of Thrones* while I ponder, "Do I want chips? No, I want cookies. No, I want ice cream. Ooooohhh, how about ice cream on cookies? Oh wait, I don't have chocolate sauce so that won't work!" You get my point. If I don't *clearly* decide that I will have a warm, raspberry-filled donut right now, then ... I won't have a donut, and I will be condemned to a life on the couch wondering why I don't have more donuts in my life.

Let's get back to your actual goals now. Here are a few questions you can ask yourself to help get the creative juices flowing about what you truly want out of life.

What things do you notice about your life when you are content (happy)?

What are three words that represent what you want out of life?

Define those three words, and then describe why those ideas and principles are critical to your life's work.

- Why are you here?
- What is your mission in life?
- How do you want to be remembered when your closest friends and family give your eulogy?
- How do you want to lead by example, especially with your kids? Why are those ideals the ones you want to exemplify?
- What do you want your legacy to be when you leave this world?
- Who do you want to influence, and how do you want to influence them?
- What people are there with you and supporting you while you do this work?

- By when do you want to incorporate these principles into your life?

This exercise is very simple and very challenging. It will take time to really consider these ideas. If you visit this work every day for a month, you will see that it will morph and become more clear over time. As I said above, this process takes dedication and contemplation, but in the end, it *will* bring clarity to your life's purpose. Remember, without clarity of purpose, there is no intention, and if there is no intention, there is no hope of achievement.

ALIGNMENT

Goal-setting is great, and the lack thereof is definitely one of the bigger roadblocks, so let's take this a step further. If there is no goal, it is very likely we don't have clear direction. If we don't have clear direction, there can be no alignment. If there is no alignment, there is no integrity and if there is no integrity, there is no action. I know there's a lot to unpack in those statements, so let me explain.

Alignment simply means that our actions, words, and energy are all working in tandem toward a common goal. When we are not consciously aligned, we roam aimlessly toward an ambiguous purpose. We become easily distracted, easily knocked off track, and easily influenced by others.

The reality is that we are all aligned with something. The key is to move from an unconscious alignment toward a directed, intentional alignment. As we do the work of self-exploration, we begin to see what we are currently aligned with versus what we want to be aligned with. Then we can create meaningful goals. When we connect with a goal at this level, we begin to direct our daily actions in a way that naturally supports our mission. Almost magically, the world begins to shift and align with our goal as well. It is a beautiful thing.

What we align with becomes what we commit to, and the world provides to us what we are committed to. The only worrisome part is that the world indiscriminately provides to us what we are truly committed to. So, if we are aligned with, and committed to, making money, we will make money. We will instinctively be on the lookout for moneymaking opportunities, and money will nearly fall in our lap. On the flip side, if we *say* we are committed to making money, but we are actually aligned with, and committed to, scarcity, then we find only lack. No matter how many positive affirmations we rehearse every day, we always reap what we sow on an energetic level. Remember that our core beliefs are what drive our train, so it becomes imperative that we find out what we really believe about ourselves (not what we want to believe) if we want to change the world with intention.

INTEGRITY

The Oxford Languages dictionary has two definitions for integrity.

First definition: The quality of being honest and having strong moral principles; moral uprightness.

Second definition: The state of being whole and undivided.

While I understand the concept behind the first definition, I believe that honesty and moral uprightness are actually *byproducts* of integrity. One cannot have honesty without integrity. The second definition comes from a much deeper and more profound place. It describes a powerful internal alignment.

Have you ever met someone who knows exactly what they want out of life? They seem to have this rulebook they follow and when they notice something that does or doesn't align with their mission, they take action. These people tend to be more direct and decisive. Yet they are also flexible and willing to change quickly if needed. How the heck do they do that? I'll tell you how—they actually do have a rulebook. It's an internal compass that is aligned with meaningful life goals. That is integrity!

By following their rulebook, they are able to save time and energy that would otherwise be wasted on contemplating decisions that don't really matter. They free up a ton of energy that they can now focus on the more important work at hand.

Integrity is the result of a conscious awareness of what we are aligned with. We know what we need/want, and we just do it. No one can knock us off course and we find steadfastness.

Integrity is an extremely powerful and sacred word. It is a representation of how well we are aligned with our purpose in life. If we are unaware of what we are aligned with, we cannot have integrity, and if we don't have integrity, it becomes impossible to move forward in our life with power and consistency. Therefore, we lose the ability to change the world with intention.

What might we say when a cop pulls us over and asks if we know why he did? The answer to this question acts like a mirror for our integrity. If we are consciously aligned with honesty, then we have no choice in our answer. Because we are aware of our commitment to honesty, we speak the truth. Integrity doesn't take a break, even if it might get us in trouble. Integrity holds us accountable for our actions, and it creates a sense of personal responsibility to do the right thing. This is why a lack of integrity becomes a huge roadblock. Without integrity, we have no compass to guide us when life takes a left turn.

If we are in integrity, we can find contentment, courage, power, consistency, and confidence. When we lack integrity, we find one of the biggest roadblocks to self-actualization and, therefore, one of the biggest roadblocks to changing the world with intention: aimlessness.

Without self-awareness, there is no alignment, which means there is no clarity of purpose, which ultimately means there is no integrity. There is no "there." All that is left is an eternity of wandering until one day you lie on your deathbed and wonder what the hell you did with all that time.

It is time to get crystal clear on what you want in this short life, and it's time to get crystal clear on why that is so important to you. Take control of your life through self-discovery, purpose, goal-setting, internal alignment, and integrity, and find your unwavering knowing of the powerful human being you are.

I'll end this segment with a brilliant quote from Stephen Covey: "When you make a commitment to yourself, do so with the clear understanding that you're pledging your integrity."

DISTRACTIONS

I understand there is a lot of information out there on this topic, so I will keep this one short. This may be one of the sneakiest roadblocks out there, because we don't even know we are doing it until after we realize we just wasted three hours staring at a little plastic box.

It's no secret that our addiction to social media, cell phones, video games, and the news is linked to feelings of inadequacy. Although these vices make us feel inadequate and fearful, we continue our addiction. After all, it's much easier to distract ourselves with doomsday stories and cat videos than it is to look in the mirror and focus on the one person who really matters: us!

Of course, the ironic part is that our distractions seem like the key to relaxing and creating some semblance of happiness in our life. However, in the long run, these distractions rob us of the energy we require to dig within and create the change that will actually bring forth happiness and contentment. Life may feel easier as we veg out, but ultimately, it takes way more energy to constantly suppress our greatness than it does to realize it.

You have greatness within you, even if you feel like you are the only person who didn't go to Europe this year. Stop taking yourself so seriously, and remember that every person on the news, at your work, or in your news feed (including yourself), is completely full of shit! We all are. Lighten up, unplug from the news, social media, and work gossip, and focus on yourself. You've earned it! You do you, in the best way you can.

If you are serious about doing you in the best way and creating the intentional life you deserve, take control and find your purpose. Knowing your purpose will bring alignment and integrity into your life, which gives you tremendous power. Goals and tasks become crystal clear, and distractions are no longer needed. You may even find energy within yourself when you thought there was none. Your purpose fuels your ambition and is essential to creating the life of your dreams.

CHAPTER 5

LACK OF PHYSICAL AWARENESS

*"To keep the body in good health is a duty…
otherwise we shall not be able to keep our
mind strong and clear."*

—Buddha

A HEALTHY BODY doesn't always equate to a healthy mind,
but a healthy mind usually equates to a healthy body.

That's not to say that in order to have a healthy mind, we
must also have a perfect body. But when our mind is healthy
and happy, we tend to offer up the same care for our body. Like
so many aspects of our life, it's about being conscious about
our choices. What are we eating, how much are we eating, how

often do we work out, what good habits do we support, and what bad habits do we cut? I wholeheartedly believe that as our soul grows, so too does our desire to maintain our physical body. After all, it is our only vessel in this life.

The physical body has a direct correlation to our energy, our mental state, and our ability to change the world. A healthy state of mind tends to lead us toward the creation of a healthy body. Additionally, when we take care of our body, it positively affects our ability to create the life we desire. I recognize that this segment will probably raise a few eyebrows, and I am OK with that. I cannot write this book without talking about physical health and our relationship to physical appearance as it relates to our ability to change the world with intention. I am not trying to judge or make anyone feel bad. I am simply stating my beliefs about this topic.

I can't state it any simpler that this:

The way we care for our body and our appearance is a reflection of how we care for our soul.

They go hand in hand. Aligned people can see themselves only as healthy, and they work every day toward the healthiest version of themselves.

If we trash our body with drugs and alcohol, it may be an indication our soul is stifled or unsettled. If we beef up so everyone will look at us, our soul may long for connection. If we eat uncontrollably, our soul may feel empty or unfulfilled. If we micromanage every piece of food we put into our body and worry about everything we eat, our soul may be fearful or anxious. When we have balance in our body and when we dress in a way that makes us feel good, we have confidence (not arrogance) in our body, and our soul is free to explore and thrive.

Our physical appearance (in the ways we can control) is a result of our choices, and our choices are a result of what is happening within us. Our physical appearance gives clues to the outside world about who we are and what we ascribe to. Punk, jock, skater, hippie, businessman, tough guy, biker, princess, emo, heartthrob, and so on. All these terms are a type of "book cover." It takes a lot of work to perfect any one of these styles. We all put great energy into carefully crafting our covers. We are nonverbally telling a story. Our outward appearances are exquisite works of art and much more revealing than we want to admit.

No matter where we are on the physical spectrum, we are all doing our best. This is not about beating ourselves up or feeling bad about where we are currently. What really matters is the *why*. When we know why we act, dress, or eat a certain way, we have choice and, therefore, we have power. When we are in alignment with our true self, we know why we do these things.

While reading the remainder of this chapter, I ask that you focus more on *why* you do the things you do so you can create awareness around your choices. That is the birthplace of an intentional life.

OUR RELATIONSHIP TO FOOD AND EATING

Let me start out by saying I am not a nutritionist and I am not going to recommend any dieting tips. That is your work.

I believe every body type and lifestyle need slightly different tweaks to make them run efficiently. With that said, there are known tips that obviously make sense, and I will touch on a few of those. Rather than preaching about the end-all, be-all diet, I intend to share some of my story and relate that to how our internal happenings dictate our relationship with food and our eating habits.

For starters, if we are what we eat, it would make sense that our health starts with what we put into our body. Additionally, our choices are a reflection of our state of mind. As we become mentally aware in our day-to-day life, we become physically aware. When we are physically and mentally aware, we begin to understand the connection between our emotions, the food we eat, and how that food interacts with our body. When we understand this concept, we gain the ability to make conscious choices about what, when, where, and why we eat.

What are you eating for breakfast, lunch, and dinner? Why do you eat those things? Do you eat them because they give you instant gratification, or do you eat them because they feed your body? Do you eat those things to fill a void, or do you eat them to fill up your tank? Do you eat them in spite of your inner wisdom, or do you eat them because of your inner wisdom? Do you eat more than you should, or do you eat slowly until you are perfectly full?

I would like to think that I lead a healthy lifestyle when it comes to my food choices. That was not always the case. To this day, I still have my moments of weakness. I will say that I enjoy the occasional drink, I love sugar, and I know that fried food is delicious. I also know the consequences of eating these things compared to the benefits they offer. Through awareness and intention, I get to choose whether or not to eat these foods, and I choose how much I eat. The difference between younger me and today me is *choice*.

I do still get out of whack now and then, and I must consciously recommit to what I want out of life. A healthy body is one important aspect of my highest self. So when I slip, I don't beat myself up or shame myself. I find my fortitude, and I fall back into my dedication toward my highest being. I reshape my mental landscape and my body. Then healthy eating habits follow suit.

I won't sit here and say that you should never drink alcohol or eat sugar or fried food. I am not here to preach that you should avoid all the fun foods. What I am saying is that when we are aware of our body and how we interact with food, we gain the ability to make conscious choices, knowing full well the benefits and the drawbacks of those choices. That is a life of *intention* rather than a life of *dictation*. And when we make intentional choices about our physical body, we look great and people will take notice!

Food is everywhere in our society. It's simply too easy to eat poorly these days. By shrugging off this responsibility, we keep ourselves trapped in a destructive cycle in which we feel bad because we eat poorly and we eat poorly because we feel bad.

After my parents were divorced when I was eight, I grew up with fast food as my main diet. My mom did cook from time to time, and she did want us to eat right. She was just very busy.

She was going to school, working, and raising three kids. I don't blame her at all. With that said, when I graduated high school, I had no idea how bad this food was making me feel. I felt like crap all the time, so I didn't know any different. I was completely unaware of how low my energy was and of how much it was affecting my state of mind.

All through college, I ate and drank whatever I wanted. For the first year and half, my crazy fast metabolism kept me skinny, but that can only last for so long. Right around my twentieth birthday, I went from 185 pounds to 215 in about six months! That's thirty pounds in six months! Over the next twelve years, I never dipped below 215 pounds.

Fortunately for me, I married a woman who comes from the opposite end of the spectrum. She brought a new perspective to my life about my relationship with food. In all honesty, for years, I thought she ate "too healthy." Once when we were dating, I had to get up early and go to work. I was building fences at the time, and it was a very physical job. I woke up late and asked if she would throw a lunch together for me really quick. I got dressed quickly, and on my way out the door she handed me a clear, gallon-sized ziploc. To my dismay, the bag was filled with about a half pound of almonds and one whole apple. As we were still new to dating, I thanked her for my "lunch" and left. Needless to say, I ate fast food that day. When it came to food, my general mindset was something like, "Where is the fun in almonds and an apple?"

A few years after I graduated college, my weight began to spike. Not surprisingly, it spiked during a time when I was feeling very unfulfilled. I wasn't interested in doing any work on myself. Personal development wasn't even on my radar. I was bored, directionless, unmotivated, and just going through the motions. One day I woke up, stepped onto the scale, and realized that I weighed just under 240 pounds. I remember looking at the scale and saying to myself, "Wow man, you're fat. You are not taking care of yourself. It's time for a change!"

So, that is what I did. I made a conscious choice to eat healthier. My wife and I worked together to cook healthier dinners, and we ate out less. This new commitment enabled me to stay between 210 and 215 for about eight or nine years. At six-foot-five, I was fine with that. I didn't see a problem, and maybe there was no problem. However, once I started really digging into my mindset, I began to realize there was still a lot of work to do.

After reading *Tools of Titans* by Tim Ferriss, I partook in a three-day fast. Then I very slowly reintroduced foods. This way, I could see how every food I ate made me feel, both during and after eating it. I noticed how hard sugar and alcohol are on my body. I learned how vegetables curb my appetite and make me feel more energetic. I learned how processed carbs make me lethargic and spike my cravings for sugar and more processed carbs. Ultimately, I learned that

we must create a healthy body to know what it feels like to have an unhealthy body.

To be honest, at this time in my life, I actually enjoyed the game and the sacrifices. My body and my choices were reflecting the work I was doing on my inner self. I recognized that if I was to achieve what I wanted out of this life, my daily choices must reflect that work. Sometimes it feels like a sacrifice to eat healthy and make difficult choices, but most of the time, what I eat is simply a reflection of what is going on inside.

My intention with this new diet had nearly nothing to do with weight loss. My intention wasn't to look good so I could turn heads. Rather, I just wanted to feel healthy and operate at my highest level. Of course, our actions have natural consequences, and the weight did fall off—fast. I started losing weight so quickly that I almost went to the doctor. I went from 215 to 185 in about three months (half the time it took for me to gain the weight in college!). Then, when I hit 185, the weight stopped coming off, and my body hit equilibrium. More important than the numbers, though, is how I feel.

I share this story as an example of how our mental state shapes our life. When we think healthy thoughts, we eat healthy foods. When we eat healthy foods, we feel good, and when we feel good, we look good! It's a superb cycle.

OUR RELATIONSHIP WITH PHYSICAL ACTIVITY

This section is straightforward. When our body is tight, lethargic, and unhealthy, so goes our mind—period. Physical activity stimulates the brain and our body. It may seem counterintuitive that the more energy we expend, the more energy we possess, but in my experience I have much more energy when I move regularly. It doesn't really matter how I move, just as long as I get some real movement every day. Sometimes I play basketball, sometimes I do yoga, sometimes I play softball, sometimes I ride my bike, sometimes I ski, and sometimes I play with my kids. No matter what the activity is, when I expend energy, it seems to actually create more. Not to mention, my body feels looser and ready to tackle each day. When I am regularly active, I am more focused, I feel better, and I look better.

Conversely, while it absolutely takes energy to stay active, let's not kid ourselves here. It takes a lot of energy to maintain the opposite lifestyle as well. It takes a lot of brainpower to hold our daily stresses in our body. It takes a lot of energy to come up with excuses as to why we should just take it easy. It takes energy to beat ourselves up over our repeated poor choices. Perhaps most importantly, it takes a ton of energy for our body to simply function day to day when it's working inefficiently. Ultimately, the campaigns I just listed rob us of much-needed energy that we could be using to make our lives better in so many ways.

I believe that the reason we have feel like we have more energy when we exercise is because our bodies as a whole run more efficiently when we allow our brains to unwind through physical activity and when we allow our bodies to release pent-up energy and stress. It's not that exercise creates more energy; it's just that regular maintenance allows our body to dispense our precious energy on the most important things.

During my junior year of high school, I had a really rough breakup with my first long-term girlfriend. I was so distraught about this breakup that it was all I could think about all day, every day. However, over time I began to notice an emerging pattern. When I went to basketball practice, she didn't even cross my mind. I was free from my destructive thoughts for two to three hours. Not only that, but after practice, I was tired and I didn't have the mental capacity to fixate on the problems anymore. It was fantastic! That's when I realized I could either put energy into my basketball game, or I could put energy into fixating on a breakup. It may not have been a completely conscious choice at the time, but nonetheless, I chose the former.

Physical activity breaks the cycle of our daily patterns and starves our ability to fixate on problems. Without this opportunity to tune out and just be, we get into a cycle called a *rut*. Eventually that rut becomes a chasm and when that happens, our soul begins to wither and die. That's when we begin to eat more and work out less, stress more and relax less, drink more and smile less. Stagnation is a huge roadblock toward changing the world with intention. Our souls desire to be free and to play. It's in our DNA. When we stifle our physical being, we suffer.

Last, I would like to point out that physical activity is going to look different for everyone. Heck, it may even look different for you today versus a year from now. It's a spectrum, and no two people are alike. You may be 300 pounds overweight, so you start with a daily walk around the block, but that simple act means something to your body and your soul. You may be a top-tier athlete, so you choose to connect with your workout in a new way. That means something to your body and your soul.

Where we start is irrelevant. What matters is our intention and our desire to become the best version of ourselves.

Everyone can work with what they have been given to make their body operate at their personalized peak condition. That peak condition looks different for everyone, but it is a peak (meaning as good as you can possibly do) nonetheless.

I am convinced that when we healthfully work toward a better physical being, we feel confident and energized and we show up in the world as a shining star. If we feel beautiful, we show up in the world as beautiful. We can't fake this kind of confidence through practicing Stuart Smalley's Daily Affirmations in a mirror. No, we can achieve this level of confidence only through the act of actually doing the work toward our best self.

PRESENTING OURSELVES TO THE WORLD

"Don't judge a book by its cover." While I would agree that you can't judge an entire book by its cover, the cover actually does have plenty of tells about what's inside. From a human standpoint, our outward appearance, whether our weight, our hair, our clothing, our posture, our habits, or how we talk to others, reflects what is happening inside. The clues we show on our "book cover" may offer insights into both desired and undesired traits about who we believe ourselves to be. We are always giving away clues about who we are.

Of course, there are some things we do not have control over—skin color, the shape of our face, a birthmark, or how tall we are, for example. But that is not what I am talking about here. I am talking about what we do have control over. Our physical health, our habits, our routines, how we dress, our posture, our relationship to our bodies, our relationship to working out and moving, our energy level, what we eat, how we address other people, and whether or not we get dressed and do our hair even when we know we don't have to leave the house that day. How we make these choices exemplifies and reflects what is going on inside of us. We are brilliant beings, and there is a reason (conscious or subconscious) why we choose to look the way we do and why we present ourselves the way we do.

Think about a time when you went to a really nice restaurant. When the plate arrived at your table, what did you expect? I don't know about you, but I expect to see a beautiful plate that has lots of color and is put together in an almost artistic fashion. Now, that food could taste like total crap, but our mind is much more likely to assume the food tastes great just because it looks great. As the adage says, "We eat with our eyes first."

This is true for our physical appearance as well. It may seem shallow at first glance, but we all have a physical presence, and every day we have the gift of deciding what our presence looks like. Once again, this is going to look different for everyone. If someone is framing houses, it wouldn't make any sense for them to show up in a freshly pressed suit every day. However, it might make sense for that person to show up in a company shirt that is clean and free of rips and tears.

The point I want to get across is that we always bring a presence with us, everywhere we go. It's time to get intentional in what your presence looks like. Are you exuding confidence, arrogance, sheepishness, laziness, lethargy, dedication, negativity, or positivity? It is up to all of us how we approach each day, and our approach is a representation of what is happening within us.

During the coronavirus outbreak in spring of 2020, we were quarantined for eight weeks. I set an intention at the beginning of the quarantine that I would maintain my morning routine. I chose to do my hair every day, even though I knew no one would ever see it. I had no one to impress, but I wanted to maintain my mental fortitude. The simple act of taking care of my hair and getting dressed every day was a reminder that I respect myself and my appearance.

Of course, this section is not just about how we dress or do our hair. It also has to do with how we present ourselves when we interact and talk with people. How we interact with and talk to people has a huge impact on our presence. If we look, feel, and communicate confidently, we are presented with a whole different set of opportunities compared to if the opposite were true.

Ultimately, I am talking about self-respect. I'm talking about taking ownership and pride in how we show up in our world. There is nothing vain about understanding how the world views us and then making adjustments so we can present ourselves in a manner we are proud of. Pride has nothing to do with vanity, how fancy our clothes are, or how expensive our car is. Pride is an understanding that we have a place in this world as we take conscious steps to show up in an intentional way. Pride is an understanding that the way we choose to present ourselves physically is a reflection of us. Pride is taking the necessary steps to show up as the best version of ourselves every day—for no one other than ourselves! As we take pride in ourselves, so goes our physical appearance, so goes our work, so goes our family life, and so goes our soul.

Just like with our physical health, if we feel good inside, we take pride in how we look outside. When we let our physical appearance slide, it is a message to the world that we don't value ourselves. If we did truly value ourselves, we would take pride in showing up in the world intentionally. That is what this book is all about. It's about being intentional in our daily life. That includes how we dress and how we take care of our physical appearance.

I am not suggesting that you go out and buy a whole new wardrobe or spend hours looking into the mirror every morning. That is vanity. What I am suggesting is that you take a good hard look at yourself every day and ask this simple question: *How do I want to be seen in the world today?* Only then do you have the power of choice. By asking that question, you get to make an intentional decision about how to do your hair, dress, speak, and stand, rather than just mindlessly getting ready and hoping for the best.

Taking care of our physical appearance is not for everyone else. It is for us! It is an act of self-care. It will definitely draw attention, and it will get us more of what we want from others, which is great, but taking care of our physical appearance is not about them. It's about feeling good about ourselves and moving through the day with confidence.

Remember, a healthy body doesn't always equate to a healthy mind, but a healthy mind does nearly always equate to a healthy body. Begin by looking inward and changing from the inside out. As your soul grows, so too will the desire for a healthy body and a healthy image. It's time for your outward presentation to match your inner beauty.

LACK OF SLEEP

It makes sense that when we take on too much, we look for ways find more time. Unfortunately, one of the first things that gets cut is sleep. It has almost become a mantra that we should wake up early and work late. That's how we crush the competition! Obviously, giving up sleep will give us more time and therefore may increase our bottom line. However, there is a cost to everything.

A simple Google search for "benefits of sleep" and "drawbacks for lack of sleep" will bring up some consistent data about how important sleep is to our well-being and our ability to change the world with intention.

I am not saying that waking up early is bad. Some people like to wake up early, and they feel better when they do. Some people wake up after six hours of sleep and feel great. Others (like me) need a solid eight to eight-and-a-half hours of sleep every night to feel best. I'm not here to speculate what the exact amount of sleep should be for every person. What I am saying is that everyone needs sleep, and I can guarantee that very few, if any, can operate at a level that promotes their highest self after four hours of sleep each night.

As humans, we don't have the bandwidth to trade sleep for money and still have the energy to create an intentional existence. At some point, something's gotta give, and true contentment is usually one of the first things to go. Personally, when

I don't get enough sleep, I feel slow, unmotivated, grumpy, moody, unfocused, and even depressed. I can feel it in my soul when I am running low on sleep. When I am tired, I just don't have the energy to be the person I want to be. My mind is sluggish and slips into autopilot at the drop of a hat. I can still function and get work done, but my emotions are all over the place and I have a hard time getting into a rhythm. On the other hand, I have also found that when I get a good night's sleep, I feel motivated, focused, productive, happier, and emotionally stable, and I retain the ability to make conscious choices throughout the day.

It takes energy to think, and it takes a lot of thinking to lead an intentional life. Therefore, sleep is an imperative component to fuel those intentional thoughts. As much as we may want to deny our need for sleep so we can get a few more hours in the day, I guarantee that a healthy night's sleep is the cornerstone of a happy and productive existence. Although that extra sale or that new car may be pretty sweet, in my opinion, there is nothing sweeter than waking up on the right side of the bed after a solid night's sleep.

Your body is your one and only vessel, and it is brilliant. So it makes sense that you should take exceptional care of it. Your body is brilliant, and if you are willing to listen, it will tell you when to get more sleep, when to switch up your diet, when to exercise, and when to keep doing what you are doing. If something makes you feel bad, stop it. If you feel lethargic, move more or get more sleep. If you feel hungry, eat more. If you feel great, keep it up! The key is to take pride in your body and become present with it. After all, it is your temple, and taking care of it is an absolute necessity if you intend to change the world.

CHAPTER 6

FEAR

"The cave you fear to enter holds the
treasures that you seek."

—Joseph Campbell

WE HAVE BEEN DISCUSSING many types of roadblocks in the past chapters. There is a lot of information in there, but if you want a more simplified idea of what really holds us back in life, I can summarize it in one word: *fear.*

Behind nearly everything we have manifested in our life is this sneaky little guy named Fear. It's not that fear is bad or good; it's just important to recognize that fear is there. Fear serves us in many forms. Fear has influenced our lifelong shadows, and it still influences many of our daily decisions. In turn, this reinforces our belief systems. So essentially, our life is run by fear, because our belief systems and shadows are shaped by our most deeply held fears.

Ultimately, we become so good at running on autopilot, which means our fears and worries dictate our decisions and life circumstances through unconscious choices, that we become addicted to our own fears. I know this sounds crazy, but there is something comforting about being engulfed in drama and fear.

Why would one want to settle into fear? Maybe fear, worry, and drama are so common in our day-to-day lives that they simply feel like home. Think about it this way. I live in Colorado, and we have a few big snowstorms that come through every year. Every time a big snowstorm is on its way, the news can't stop talking about it. For days, they mention it before every commercial break, and the weather person is on twice as much. The news stations don't do this because they are so excited about snow. (Well, maybe they are.) Rather, they promote this big event because the discussion triggers viewer fears, which increases ratings, which sells more ad space. They don't stop talking about it, because they know everyone wants to feed into the drama of the whole event. And people are willing to pay to get their drama fill. We may not be paying money directly to the news stations, but we are paying in time and attention as we continue to watch.

I find it kind of weird to think about, but there is something about the drama and worry surrounding an impending storm that comforts us and makes us feel warm and cozy. I'm not a psychologist, so I won't pontificate (fancy word alert) too much as to why this is the case, but I will state that this behavior is a reality.

TV AND FEAR

TV content is profitable only when people tune in and stay tuned in to content. That is how ad space is sold. To sell the most ad space, TV programmers simply identify the content that our society enjoys most and then they play programming that panders to our common denominators. Simply put, if they pander to what we are most addicted to, we tune in more and they sell more ad space. Pretty simple, really, and it probably doesn't come as a surprise to most of us. The funny thing is that even with this common knowledge, we still tune in. We (myself included) still feed the monster that feeds us drama, fear, worry, and panic. I love human psychology!

As I see it, there are three major components of entertainment that are the most profitable. We love drama, fear, and tension, and we are more than willing to donate our precious and limited free time to these programs that provide our much-needed fix.

The number one most popular category is overly dramatic shows (dramas) and reality TV. These are all over primetime, Netflix, and Hulu. These shows create wild emotional swings for the viewer, and we *love* it! Make me cry, yes! Make me mad, yes! Make me anxious, yes! Allow me to judge, yes! These shows tend to have a somber and depressing undertone that reminds us "at least my life isn't that screwed up." They are jam-packed with opportunities for us to judge and comment on the behavior of others. They keep us distracted from our own lives and our own problems. These shows provoke tension that is sourced from deeply held fears or shadows within us. Dramas play on our insecurities and create emotional swings when we watch. And we absolutely love it! We tweet about it, we talk about it at the water cooler, and we dissect it. Give me drama or give me death!

The second most popular category is action and horror shows. This includes alternate realities, over-the-top fight scenes, big guns, explosions, revenge, death, destruction, utopian societies, and superheroes. I can almost hear Tim "The Tool Man" Taylor grunting as I write that last sentence. These shows exemplify some ominous change of circumstances, and a hero must save us all from ourselves or from this horrible fate. These shows make us think things like, "Oh my God! Can you imagine if this actually happened?"

When coronapocalypse hit in 2020, the most popular shows on Netflix were not shows about how to become more present in the face of fear. They had nothing to do with mindfulness or how to stay level-headed during a crisis. Rather, the most popular movies being watched when coronavirus became real were *Outbreak, 2012, 3022,* and *Pandemic.* C'mon people! We have a real pandemic on our hands, and all we can think to do is scare the bejesus out of ourselves and feed into our fear by watching a bunch of movies about how life as we know it ends in the wake of a horrible pandemic? I'll say it again. There is something comforting about being a part of this extreme drama. We love the fear. Perhaps it's because we live in this fearful place so much that it's like a warm hug in uncertain times.

The third category is news shows. This is the most insidious of them all, because the news appears to be based on the real world. This also includes sports news. You might say, "How dare you? Sports news is cheeky and fun." Well, just like regular news, sports news is intended to create drama and, therefore, emotionally charge viewers to create fanaticism. That's what sells ad space!

If we don't tune into the news all day, every day, then how do we know about all the things that are threatening our way of life, our safety, and our country, and more importantly, how do we protect ourselves from it all? It is our civic duty to be fully informed on what is coming for us next, right?

I have often been ridiculed for not following the news religiously. How do I know what is happening in the world? How do I keep up on the war efforts overseas? How do I know what I am supposed to be afraid of, outraged over, and worried about? Great questions, but I'm going to answer with another question. Now that you know about all these things, what are you going to do about them?

I'm not saying that we should shun the rest of the world and forget about everyone but ourselves, but what I am saying is that we have a limited amount of brainpower and a limited amount of energy. What we focus on regularly becomes our reality. If we are constantly barraged with all the bad things in this world, all the bad people doing bad things, all the wars, and all the bad stuff that's ready to come get us, what does our reality look like? I don't think I need to answer that question.

The news shows understand that we want the dirt and the drama, and more importantly, we want to know what to fear. So they play stories over and over and fixate on topics that they know make us feel fearful, worried, angry, or judgmental. "Wait, my Fitbit is controlling my brain? No ... don't go to a commercial! Fine ... I'll wait. I gotta hear this!"

I do catch flak for not watching the news, but at the end of the day I am very well informed about important events that directly affect me, or issues I plan to do something about. I don't see that as sticking my head in the sand; I see that as being efficient and focused. By focusing on what I can control, I conserve the needed energy to actually do something about it. I don't have the brainpower to reflect on and solve all the world's problems, and neither do you. That is why we elect other people whose job it is to focus on that stuff for us. When we focus on everything, we become overwhelmed, then we panic, then we shut down and get nothing done.

I'm not trying to trash TV or say we shouldn't watch. It's too juicy for that. Rather, I am saying that, through awareness, we gain more control over what we consume and why we consume that information. Awareness allows us to gain more control over our life. When we consciously understand what a show has to offer, how a show affects us emotionally, and why we want to watch it, we have the power of choice—the power to choose what comes into our awareness. Conversely, when we mindlessly sit in front of the boob tube and zone out, we are slaves to the content that our subconscious absorbs. It's all about awareness and consciousness.

Ultimately, the most popular content watched by Americans is a projection of what we value, and it's obvious that we value fear. Fear of abandonment, fear of failure, fear of death or injury, fear of loss (freedom, relationships, jobs), fear of differing opinions, fear of acceptance, and on and on. These shows create a space for us to judge (ourselves and others), dispute, blame, hate, cry, project, cower, zone out, and ignore our own life. Just tune in and forget about yourself. TV's got your back.

Unfortunately, the more we fixate on drama, whether through TV, conversations with friends, or internet searches, the more we train our brains to live in fear. You have all heard the example of the new car. When I buy a new car, I all of a sudden notice every car that is just like mine. The world didn't change, but my focus did. This is true for every facet of our life. If we focus on drama, tension, bad news, and doomsday stories, then our life is filled with the same. With TV being so easily accessible, it is more important now, more than ever, to create awareness around what we are taking in. If we want to change the world with intention, it's time to get very intentional about what we are feeding our soul.

FEAR AND CHOICE

Fear itself doesn't block us from changing the world with intention. After all, fear isn't even real. It's simply a projection that we create within ourselves, and that projection is what robs us of our ability to choose how we show up in the world. The roadblock actually stems from a lack of awareness as to why we do what we do.

Although fear can hold us back from achieving our true potential, we must also recognize the potential for positive consequences. Fear can be a great teacher. Here's the catch: Although our fears can create positive results such as saving our life when we are in danger, our complacency in understanding the fears within us hampers our ability to understand our options. The real benefits and lessons from our fears don't show themselves until we become aware of what is happening in our subconscious.

When I was growing up, it seemed like I heard a repetitious message that I was unprepared and making stupid mistakes. It felt like I heard this message from my parents, my teachers, my friends, my coaches, everyone. Whether that was the actual message or not is irrelevant, because that is the message I *heard*. Of course, that is all that matters in the end. When I became an adult, this story led to a deep-rooted shadow belief that I will always let people down through stupid mistakes brought on by a lack of preparation. Over time, this shadow led to a fear that when I let someone down, they would judge me and they wouldn't like me anymore. My horrible secret (that I always screw everything up) would be revealed to the world, and I would be shown for the fraud I was. I felt like I was destined to continually screw things up and roam this world alone. Keep in mind that this idea was buried in the back of my subconscious, so I was unaware of this program.

Ironically, the fear of driving people away was actually what tended to drive people away. I never, ever, ever saw myself as a perfectionist, but guess what? I had become one. Crazy! I would rake myself over the coals for any mistake, and I would lament about what an idiot I was. It eventually got to the point where I was working against myself in a major way. I was putting so much energy into making sure I didn't screw up that I was putting no energy into actually not screwing up. That makes sense, right?

This exemplifies how fear can create problems while at the same time creating gifts. This fear paralyzed me at times. This fear sent me into fits of depression and self-deprecating behavior, so it's not too surprising that this belief was at the heart of my suicidal thoughts. On the flip side, without perfectionism, my business would not be nearly as tailored and efficient as it is today. Without the fear of mistakes, I wouldn't have become so dedicated to absorbing knowledge as a teacher, realtor, or speaker.

One day I woke up and realized that although my fear had created many gifts in my life, I had been running on autopilot. I looked up and saw that this shadow belief was driving my train. I recognized that to regain my power, I had to reintegrate this fear. I finally understood that, through awareness, I could regain the option to choose, and I was able to leverage this fear into serving my highest purpose. I can now appreciate the gifts this shadow has bestowed upon me, and I can regulate the destructive behaviors. However, without intentional work around this disowned piece of myself, I would have been destined to sit on autopilot while my choices were dictated by my subconscious.

FEAR AND BRAVERY

Oftentimes, fear can keep us safe. Without fear, we would be prone to repeating stupid mistakes over and over. Many times, great change in our life is catalyzed by fear. A fear of poverty may create an unstoppable drive that generates great wealth. A fear of inadequacy may create a drive within us to change the world so we can be recognized. A fear of loneliness may create a strong drive in us to create relationships and bring groups of people together. All these things can be great, and fear is the driving force behind them. However, they can also be very destructive.

To change the world with intention, we have to come from a place of awareness and acceptance, and this includes awareness and acceptance of our fears. Blindly running into a building without a healthy fear and awareness is foolishness, not bravery. Running into a burning building after assessing the situation and acknowledging fear is bravery. Through awareness, we reintegrate our fears, which then allows us to tap into our power.

Resistance to fear most commonly shows up in one of two ways: either blind bravery or some form of shutting down. Whether we freeze or whether we run toward a burning building without a second thought, that action can be destructive if it is devoid of choice.

Some people are more comfortable with the idea of fear and may be more prone to seek out things they fear and address those fears head-on. Others are paralyzed by fear so they choose to do nothing. Regardless of how we react to fear, the power is found when we consciously recognize and then address it through awareness. If your goal is to change the world with intention, you must understand that overcoming fear is about awareness and acceptance rather than resistance.

Just like so many aspects of our life, bravery is born through awareness. People may have jumped out of planes, fought in an octagon, run into battle, or swum with the sharks. We might blindly believe these people are brave, or we may even go so far as to say they have no fear. I can guarantee that even though they tout their favorite "No Fear" shirt from 1997, they definitely have fear. What I will say is that unless they are consciously aware of why they are participating in those activities, their shadow is running the show and they have no choice in the matter. Operating on any level without the opportunity of choice is not bravery; it is servitude.

There is no bravery without fear. Bravery recognizes fear and proceeds through conscious action. Remember that bravery is *not* the antithesis to fear. Bravery works *in tandem* with fear. Love and acceptance are the antitheses to fear. When we find love for the things we most fear, we can accept those fears as part of our life. Then we begin to find a stillness and a steadfastness that produces bravery.

Fear is present in our life every day, like it or not. Much of what we do is an attempt to feed, cover up, or run away from some form of fear. Social media, alcohol, drug abuse, dare deviling, politics, news, and judging are all easy ways to distract ourselves. Ultimately, the only escape from fear is awareness and personal development. Once you begin the work of developing yourself, you have started down a path that empowers a brave new you.

CHAPTER 7

LACK OF HELP

*"One of the biggest deficits in life is the
inability to ask for help."*

—Robert Kiyosaki

OUR FINAL ROADBLOCK is just as important as any other
we have covered so far. This roadblock can slow or completely
stall the growth process. I am, of course, talking about doing all
of this on your own. I can't say it any simpler than this.

Don't do this on your own!

In the story I shared about my own relationship with perfectionism, you may have guessed that I didn't figure it all out on

my own. If so, you were right. There were many forces at play as I came to the realization that I had actually become a perfectionist. I am always working with a coach or therapist. Just having another set of eyes on our life can bring awareness to things we are completely blind to. Also, through meditation and a willingness to listen, I was able to tap into and get guidance from the universe, God, Superconscious, whatever you want to call it. That force is always there for us. That is the nature of what/ who it is. The problem arises when we stop listening to our trusted advisors and when we lose our connection to universal guidance. When we proclaim that we can do this on our on our own, we easily become lost.

That's not to say that we won't ever figure out things on our own, but I can guarantee it will take way longer. Aside from taking forever, without help, we are very likely to miss out on key discoveries that can change our life. With a strong commitment to yourself and to the process, combined with a little help, you will grow so fast, and you'll feel a foot taller.

Yes, I know you have the power and the ability to figure this out all on your own. Yes, I know you believe no one knows you better than you. Yes, I know you have already figured it all out and you are done growing now. That's all great, but correct me if I'm wrong: if I asked you to tell me ten things about one of your friends that they could work on, you could probably name twelve before I finish this sentence.

We all know everything that's wrong with everyone else. The problem is that we can't see *our* stuff very well. The beautiful part is that, just like you and your friend, everyone else can see right through you. By having someone on the outside pointing out all your problems, you can streamline the process like crazy. Don't do this on your own.

There are many excuses as to why we feel we can do this on our own, and I am here to bust 'em all.

- You may not want to get help because you don't have the money. Well, what comes first: the chicken or the egg? Financial freedom or personal growth? Perhaps a little work on yourself will create more money, which will in turn create more opportunities to work with coaches.

- Maybe you don't want to get help because you are afraid of being vulnerable and you don't want someone knowing all your dirty laundry. First of all, most people can already see your dirty laundry. None of us are as clever at concealing our dark sides as we think. Second, if this is your excuse, then we have just uncovered a shadow and it's probably been affecting nearly every aspect of your life for years. Congrats! Now you can go get some help to work through that.

- Maybe you just don't want anyone to know you are broken. Perhaps you feel that if others know you are seeing a coach or, worse yet, a shrink, they will judge you. First of all, they *will* judge you (whether going to counseling or not), but just remember that their judgment is about them and not you. Second, getting help because you want to go kick some ass in this world is heroic and that is something to be proud of, not ashamed of. Own it!

There are a 1,000 more excuses, and since I said I would bust them all, I better do that. Here is the answer to every excuse: None of the excuses matter! They are just excuses. All of them. Don't do this on your own.

This is a huge project, and you need help. Time to get over yourself and find a trusted partner to walk with you on your journey. They may be with you for three months or three years. You may work with someone new every few months. It doesn't matter, as long as you are growing.

I'll leave you with this. I have had plenty of opportunities to remind myself how awesome I am and how great I am doing on my journey. Sometimes it feels like I have arrived and I have it all figured out. Then life reminds me that I am only just beginning. When I go into a session with a coach thinking I have nothing to work on, I almost always come out of those "What could we possibly talk about today?" sessions with some of my biggest discoveries. This work is never completed and once you catch the bug, I am confident you will be perfectly fine with that. Get the help, get another point of view, remember there is always work to do, and soak up the journey. It's the only one we have.

FEEDBACK

This section actually has less to do with getting feedback and more to do with what we do when we get feedback. It's really about listening, internalizing, and changing for the better.

Have you ever heard the popular quote, "Love yourself for who you are and never change for anyone"? Although I understand the underlying message, which is intended to empower people, I believe this unintentionally opens the door to excuses and avoiding personal responsibility toward growth.

I feel this message has become a beacon for people to cop out and simply say, "I shouldn't have to change a thing." The reality is that we actually generate contentment as we change and as we work toward becoming the best version of ourselves. Contentment comes only through the struggle.

Many times, other people can see right through our masks, and we should absolutely take into consideration what they are saying. That doesn't mean we listen to everyone equally, and blindly do whatever anyone says. It means we consider the origin of the input, we consider the credibility of the input, and then we intentionally move forward in a way that creates change toward our highest self.

I obviously agree that we should love ourselves for who we are and we should always love and appreciate ourselves for where we are in our journey. Loving ourselves every day is paramount to our personal development, and this message brings that idea to the forefront of our mind. I love that.

We have never arrived, and we can always do better! We should always be looking for ways we can grow by consistently reflecting on our weak spots. Looking for ways to improve our mind or our physical body is not a sign of weakness or self-deprecation. It is a sign of great strength! In fact, in order to reflect in a healthy way, we must tap into pride and self-love, and that takes confidence and strength.

While I agree that the change should most definitely be based on our own objectives, other people may have wise advice about how we can change. If everyone is always telling us that we look depressed, angry, tired, annoyed, and so on, perhaps there is some truth to their feedback. Maybe we should take a moment to listen and find ways to improve so we can tap into our highest power. Once again, having an understanding that we are imperfect and understanding that we don't have all the answers are signs of courage and confidence, rather than weakness.

In the end, we should always love ourselves right where we are, but subscribing to this idea that we should never change for anyone is bull hockey. Other people can be fantastic mirrors, and therefore we need to listen from time to time. Sometimes they are self-serving or mean, and we should tell them to take a hike. But as we become more present, our ability to distinguish the messages becomes stronger and stronger. When we have integrity we know whom to listen to and what advice is worth listening to.

BREAKING THROUGH ROADBLOCKS

I could go on and on about a slew of other things that could potentially hold us back in life, but in the end I believe most inhibitors can be traced back to one or more of the items covered in the last few chapters. This is some heavy stuff, and I understand that. It's challenging to look at ourselves and admit our shortcomings, but remember that lasting change doesn't come by accident. It takes awareness, dedication, and intention.

Let's take a quick moment here to recap the major roadblocks we've covered:

- Lack of Self-Reflection
- Lack of Purpose
- Lack of Physical Awareness
- Fear
- Lack of Help

Notice the word *lack* shows up a lot when discussing roadblocks. By dodging the responsibility of self-discovery, we continue to lack in every aspect of our life. In other words, by remaining unaware, we have no other option but to live in an eternal state of lack. The only way to undo lack is to do some-/anything. As we do the work of self-exploration and discovery, lack transmutes into awareness. As our awareness grows, we gain the power of choice, and when we have the power of choice, we can change our world with intention, and when we change the world with intention, abundance and contentment follow.

In Chapter 2, I revealed my story. I have made plenty of poor choices. I have created stories that were not generating prosperity. I thought I wanted money, but I really wanted security. I thought I wanted acceptance, but I really wanted love. I thought I wanted success, but I really wanted fulfillment. I thought I was committed to many things in my life, but I eventually realized I was actually committed to the results that showed up in my life. Once I began the work to understand who I really am, I was able to discover how I got here and what I actually want out of life.

Now I realize that, at the very least, I am doing something to make my life and the world better. The ups and downs are natural, but the work is a lifestyle. I am blessed to have created the opportunity to accept and love myself, which has ultimately led to the design of a life full of joy, contentment, passion, and prosperity.

Why are you reading this book? I would venture a guess that you know you can do better. There's no shame in that. There is always something that needs to shift in all our lives. The question really becomes, why haven't you made those shifts yet? Is it because there is a price to be paid for making those shifts? Perhaps it scares you that you will "risk it all" if you just stop worrying and go after what you truly want. Maybe you fear how others will perceive you if you simply start smiling all the time. Maybe you worry that your family or friends won't love you anymore if you begin standing up for yourself. Maybe you worry that your business will fail unless you constantly stress over every detail. In all honesty, it doesn't really matter. All that matters now is that you have recognized you are an amazing being who is capable of fantastic things and you have work to do.

Remember that, as we do the work and as we become more aware about ourselves, we become more aware of our choices and the consequences of those choices. That means, from time to time, we will discover we make really poor choices. That is OK! Don't beat yourself up. Even when we screw things up, we can always fall back on the fact that we are doing the work and playing the game. Our awareness will always bring new challenges into our life, and that means we will make mistakes. But it also affords us the opportunity to analyze our choices so we can learn and grow. In the end, our mistakes become our victories. Through the simple act of trying, we cannot fail.

Theodore Roosevelt said it best:

"It is not the critic who counts; not the man who points out how the strong man stumbles, or where the doer of deeds could have done them better. The credit belongs to the man who is actually in the arena, whose face is marred by dust and sweat and blood; who strives valiantly; who errs, who comes short again and again, because there is no effort without error and short-coming; but who does actually strive to do the deeds; who knows great enthusiasms, the great devotions; who spends himself in a worthy cause; who at the best knows in the end the triumph of high achievement, and who at the worst, if he fails, at least fails while daring greatly, so that his place shall never be with those cold and timid souls who neither know victory nor defeat."

As you read on, I pose a challenge to you. Yes, *you*, the one reading this book. The rest of this book is about moving beyond where you are now. If you truly desire to move forward in your life, then it is time to do things differently. My challenge is to let go of your resistance and dedicate your life to self-discovery. I guarantee it will be the hardest thing you ever do and it will be the most rewarding thing you ever do. Stop ignoring your soul. You have the answers inside you right now. Go get a life coach, counselor, or shadow coach. Start digging into your past and learning about who you really are. Then move forward with a powerful new resolve to change the world with intention.

PART III

WORLD CHANGERS

"Yesterday I was clever, so I wanted to change the world. Today I am wise, so I am changing myself."

—Rumi

THE LAST FEW CHAPTERS, we discussed self-created roadblocks that we subconsciously build into our lives. Adhering to these roadblocks allows our ego to be right while stopping us from creating what we really want. When we succumb to the power of our ego, we get the benefit of predictability and a feeling of security, but that comes at a price of our happiness and growth. Although predictability may be enticing and comforting, it does not bring challenge, fun, happiness, joy, or contentment into our lives. I am reminded of a quote from the book *Get Out of Your Own Way* by Dave Hollis: "A ship in harbor is safe, but that's not what ships are built for." In the next few chapters, we will begin to reshape our relationship between our roadblocks and our growth. As we look to expand and move forward with intention, we will begin to look at our roadblocks as opportunities rather than obstacles in our way.

Our roadblocks are self-created; therefore, they are also self-correctable. When we are living on autopilot, we attempt to create controlled and predictable environments, which we believe will allow us to protect ourselves from risk, pain, discomfort, and fear. Ironically, we also "protect" ourselves from prosperity and growth. It's time to bravely break free from the chains of predictability and comfort and lean into the unpredictability and beauty of growth. It's time to get comfortable with being uncomfortable.

Being a world changer means that we move forward, beyond our self-limiting beliefs, and positively impact the world in our own special way. Moving forward has less to do with where we came from, and more to do with acceptance of what actually is. Once we accept what is, we give space to recognize our struggles, and we then gain the opportunity to grow as a person and powerfully impact the world.

I challenge you to let go of what you think you already know. Simply play with the idea that perhaps you don't know everything, and perhaps you are wrong about what you know about yourself and the world around you. Through your acceptance that you (and your ego) could be wrong, you open yourself up to new understandings. You don't have to blindly take these thoughts for gospel, but through a willingness to accept that you may be wrong, you at the very least become open to new possibilities. That is all it takes to begin the journey toward a new, more powerful, you.

CHAPTER 8

MOVING FORWARD

"All our dreams can come true if we have the courage to pursue them."

—Walt Disney

WHEN I SAY the word *acceptance*, what comes to mind? Sit for a moment and think about what that word means to you. Does it spark thoughts of weakness or strength? Does it seem impossible or invigorating? Does it bring up fear or ego? Just sit with it for a few minutes.

ACCEPTANCE WITHOUT ACQUIESCENCE

To some, acceptance may seem similar to giving in or getting pushed around, but to me, acceptance is a word of great power. True acceptance requires one to relinquish control and show faith. That said, there is a distinction to be made. I call it acceptance without acquiescence. This phrase is a lot more fun to say than it is easy to do.

Acceptance has been one of my most challenging struggles. It was always me versus the world. So I was in a constant state of resistance. A constant state of "Oh yeah, I'll show you!" When I heard the word *acceptance* in the past, the ideas that came to my mind were: giving in, caving, weakness, push over, and acquiescing. I saw accepting what is as a sign of weakness. As if I were just throwing my hands in the air and shouting "fine!" As a young person who felt bullied my whole life, there was no way I was going to give in. No way I was going to accept and let someone or some circumstance push me around. Rather, I embraced the idea of controlling my life and, in turn, accepted a never-ending struggle. My plan was to fight the power, prove everyone wrong, and resist anything or anyone that was not the way it "should be." Missio is a musical group from Texas, and they seem to get it: "I'll just keep throwing middle fingers in the air!"

Over time, as I played with the idea of acceptance, I began to realize what this word really means. Acceptance is about leaning into reality and deciding to work with what actually is. Acceptance is about removing resistance. Acceptance is an act of great strength and power. It takes fortitude to accept what actually is, remove resistance to what is, and then move forward with alignment and intention.

The antithesis to acceptance is resistance. When we are in

resistance, there is no solution to a problem. There is no moving forward, because our mind is focused on what "should be" rather than what "is" and what can be. Resistance bogs down our brain, distracts us, and ultimately keeps us stuck. It would make sense then, that when we remove resistance, acceptance fills the void. Then, a whole new world of possibilities opens up for us. It's a perspective shift that focuses our energy in a more productive direction.

Acceptance can be hard to explain on paper, so as I continue with this line of thought, I ask that you play with these ideas in your own life. Acceptance is a practice that can be attained only through implementation in your own life. Play with it, and find out for yourself what possibilities open up for you as you release resistance and accept what is.

Ironically, as I write this piece about acceptance I am currently in a state of resistance myself.

I woke up with a full day on the calendar. I was scheduled to do a radio interview about real estate and divorce. This was a great opportunity for me to educate my fellow realtors and attorney partners about this topic, and I was really looking forward to it. I had a basketball practice in the evening for my nine-year-old son. This was the very first practice with his new competitive basketball team, and I was so excited to get everyone together. Additionally, it was our only practice this week, and I was out the following week for travel. Long story short, I was eager for the start of the season. I was also planning to get my car towed to my friend's garage, because I had recently slid into a curb and I needed to get it to a body shop for repairs. I had a typical day filled with all sorts of activities and stresses. All this *should* have gone off without a hitch; however, reality had a different plan. Time to struggle (throat clear), I mean grow.

At 6:15 a.m., I checked my email. The first thing I saw was that all after-school activities were canceled due to a big snow storm blowing through our area. This meant our first practice of the season and our only practice this week was canceled. Some teams would get two practices this week, and we would get zero. Additionally, because I was out the next week for travel, I was going to miss our team's first practice. Remember the story at the beginning of this book? I wasn't even out of bed yet and I was already upset, bummed, shut down, and in a state of resistance. *This is garbage, and I shouldn't have to deal with all this.* I was throwing middle fingers in the air already and it was only 6:30 a.m.!

I went downstairs in a bad mood, unprepared to go through my traditional morning routine and set myself up for success. I was completely out of rhythm. Then I realized that the tow company was not working today or tomorrow. *Ahhhh! Snow!* Now I may not get my car repaired before I leave town. As I lamented about all this, I discovered one more cancelation: my much-anticipated radio spot. Now everything was really screwed! At this point, my horrible attitude took hold and I decided the best course of action was to skip the few things that might be able to help me center a bit: yoga and writing. Instead, I looked at my daily calendar. *Let's see what* else *I can't do today and find more evidence to support the "suckiness" of today.* Great idea, Dan! No writing, no yoga, canceled radio spot, canceled basketball practice... On and on I went.

Not surprisingly, I eventually lost my cool and started to yell about how snow sucks and the day was ruined. There is no silver lining, and everything *should be* different. I was in major resistance and had no qualms about letting the world know.

That's a rough start to what would have been a very promising day.

My negativity rubbed off on my family and transferred to my kids and my wife. Remember, every action has an equal reaction, and it is hard to tell how far my negative ripples would have traveled throughout that day or even through the days to come. At that moment, I was influencing the world without intention. I was influencing the world from a place of unconscious reaction. My programs and my ego were in full control.

All of a sudden and without warning, I caught myself. I don't know exactly where this moment of clarity came from, but I truly believe I was able to tap into the universe's guidance through a daily mindfulness practice. Even though I didn't practice that day, all the work on previous days was paying off. I believe that by practicing self-awareness every day, I created a rhythm that allows me to go on autopilot for only so long before my intuition (universe) steps in and says, "Hey there, what's going on?"

Even though I was still in a state of resistance, my practice allowed me to become aware of my resistance. New ideas began to flow through me. I decided that if there ever was a day to do yoga and meditation, this was one of them. I headed to my practice area and began my routine. As I quieted my mind and let go of my repeating thoughts, I began to sink into a place of deeper acceptance. Not totally there yet, but getting closer. Then I continued to calm my mind. Closer to acceptance. I tried to remove any thoughts from my head. Just be. Just be.

As I sank further into my meditation and let go of my resistance, ideas started to pop into my head. Just because the gym is closed, it doesn't mean the basketball team can't get together. Why don't I just have the basketball team over to my house instead? We can watch a Steph Curry video on ball handling and then do some drills in my basement. That would work. Even if the tow truck can't come today or tomorrow, it will come soon and my car will get fixed while I am gone. I can't drive today anyway (snow, remember), so no real harm in that. My radio show will get rescheduled, and I will probably be more prepared anyway. On top of that, I have time today to work on my "to do" list.

As soon as I stopped swimming upstream, a whole new world opened right up.

I finally realized that resistance was keeping me trapped in a narrow realm of possibilities.

Remember that acceptance is not disillusionment. Notice that I didn't begrudgingly accept that my day was ruined and pretend I was OK with it. I didn't acquiesce to the circumstances and shove my real feelings down.

Rather, I stepped into my place of power by recognizing what was happening, both in the situation and within myself. I addressed and showed compassion for my feelings of anger and frustration and accepted what was. Then I removed my resistance to the actual circumstances and created a plan that was aligned with who I really wanted to be. That is power, my friends! That is acceptance.

Have you ever been in a place of resistance like that? If you take a moment to reflect, it is kind of comical. It's as though I was hitting myself in the head with an emotional tack hammer while saying, "Stop hitting yourself in the head with a tack hammer." It's ridiculous. Trying to forcefully stop myself from resisting is a form of resistance, and it only made things worse.

In the end, resistance blocks our ability to think clearly. Our fight-or-flight response kicks in, and we say, "This sucks. I quit. Things should be different so no sense in trying." Then we take it out on the people around us and lower the energy of the world. Unless we consciously do something about our negative attitude, we propagate negativity and hurt the people we care about most (including ourselves). We all do this. We want things to be different, but guess what? They aren't. Get over it. It is what it is. Why lower the energy of the entire world, simply because you won't accept what is?

When we make the conscious choice to accept, we lower stress levels in our body and we create space to influence the world in a positive way. Then we can lead by example and raise the energy of the world. When we choose to accept, we inspire people around us with our creativity and relentless drive toward finding a better way. Then we can move forward with authority, because we have a knowing that there are endless solutions. When we choose to accept, we tap into the limitless power of the universe and we often surprise ourselves with how powerful we are. Then the world opens up to us, and we see things much more clearly. It truly is magical.

It is time to accept your life in its entirety and stop resisting what is. Even though you didn't have any control over the things that happened to you in the past, you *do* have control over how you react to them, today. It is time for you to realize you do have power and you do have answers within yourself. This is where you are; what are you going to do about it?

I know that accepting can be one of the most challenging things to do. I struggle with it every day. But I can promise that the exercise of acceptance will be well worth it. I use the word *exercise* on purpose, because it is important to remember that this is a practice and this is something that takes repetition. You are going to mess it up and that's OK. Just keep exercising that muscle, and great things will inevitably follow.

You can resist reality and block the universe's help, or you can accept and begin to tap into the answers that are right in front of you. You are amazingly powerful. Remember that you don't have to quit or give in to find acceptance. Let it go without acquiescence. You are where you are. That's a fact. What you are going to do about it is 100 percent up to you. Accept your responsibility. Accept your role moving forward. Accept that you have the answers. Accept that you have the power to change. Accept that you can rewrite your story any time you want. Then let the universe guide you as you tap into your God-given power and move forward with intention.

I started in a place of resistance and was getting absolutely nowhere. I yelled about my circumstances and lowered the energy vibration of myself and my family. I created chaos in my life and everyone around me. Then, through a spark of awareness,

I found acceptance. Through that acceptance, I tapped into my power and found the answers that brought me closer to the person I want to be. What an amazing tool acceptance is!

MINDSET

Through the art of acceptance, we welcome struggle into our life. It is a natural progression.

Once we accept where we are, once we accept that we are flawed and we can do better, we see our imperfections and then the struggle can begin. The beautiful part is that struggle will lead to growth, and growth is the root of all contentment. At least for me, there is something satisfying when I recognize a struggle, figure out a way to work through it, and ultimately grow from the experience. That is what life is all about. If we want to move forward in our life, we have to make ourselves uncomfortable and create meaningful struggle.

I was watching a documentary the other day on Taylor Swift. At one point, she mentioned that as she found success, she also found "haters." People on the internet were saying horrible things about her. Unfounded and way over-the-top things. What I love is that she said these comments and experiences took her mind to some bad places, but ultimately they were an opportunity for growth. I am sure that she has a journey in front of her as she tries to discover who she really is, just like all of us, but it appears that her mindset will ultimately lead to positive change in her life.

At the end of the day, our struggles define who we are. Our struggles have the power to crush our spirit and destroy us, or they also have the power to inspire us, reinvigorate our lives, and guide us toward new, more empowering beliefs. It's all about perspective. Perspective is a powerful thing.

ALAN'S PERSPECTIVE

Alan is a single guy in his early thirties. He is tired of dating and ready to find "the right one." He has become increasingly frustrated with the dating scene and is starting to doubt his lovability. All his friends are married or have longtime girlfriends, and he can't figure out why he can't seem to find love. One day, he meets a girl named Jackie who seems like a perfect fit for him. Unfortunately, after four months of dating, she suddenly breaks up with him. He may or may not know it, but if he so chooses, this is the opportunity he has been waiting for. This is an opportunity for self-discovery and transformation. Or, this is an opportunity for self-doubt and depression. It all depends on his perspective.

Perspective for choice 1: Here we go again. I just gave my heart to another girl, not to mention four months of my life, and she could care less. She moves on with her life, and I am left here (alone) to pick up the pieces of my broken heart. Dating sucks. Why do I even try? I'm done with women. Should I try dating men? No, I'm just done trying. I'm going to call the boys and go out and get drunk.

Perspective for choice 2:

Well that sucked! I guess she wasn't the right person for me. I wonder what I could have done differently? Actually, I think the better question is, was I in alignment with my true self when we were together? Yes, I believe I was. I could have done a few things differently, but for the most part, I was in alignment with who I want to be. If she was the right person for me, then she would have resonated with me and we would have stayed together. I am so glad I was able to figure this out in only four months. I was really falling for her, so this could have dragged out for years. I'll bet the right girl for me is just around the corner. I should call my boys so we can go out and I can continue the search.

Perspective 1 is full of deflection and denial about his role in this breakup. He has set himself up for another failure and a deeper crevasse that he will then have to climb out of. The more he denies reality and fails to look inward, the bigger his hole and the harder it is to climb out. He is blaming others, beating himself up, and looking to bury his sorrows by getting drunk with his buddies (as if that will solve his problem). Drugs and alcohol are so damaging in these scenarios. They lower our ability to shift perspective, stifle our spirit, and send us down dark rabbit holes when we are already down.

Perspective 2 may seem a bit pie in the sky—an impossibility—but it isn't. As I have said so many times, a healthy perspective comes from a place of awareness and acceptance, which stems from reflection. In scenario 2, he creates the opportunity to discover whether he was in alignment or not. Then he can adjust for the next time. That's the definition of growth. He is not perfect, but he is better. See the difference? He has more wisdom and more awareness, and with his new awareness he has created the power of choice. Even though he had no control over the breakup, he has control over his reaction and, therefore, he has control over his life.

Take a moment and let this story sink in. One event—two very different perspectives, two very different existences, and two very different results. As we look to move forward, we must remember that perspective is one of the most powerful tools we have in our tool bag.

MY PERSPECTIVE SHIFT

As I sit here and write this segment, I am in a struggle of my own. Aren't we all! My wife is recovering from ACL surgery and can't drive, cook, go up the stairs on her own, or even fix my boo-boos when I get hurt. It also means, in addition to my regular workload and family roles, I am also responsible for her chores and family roles. One of those new roles means getting the kids ready for school in the morning.

This morning, my son—who, like most nine-year-old boys, is constantly losing his stuff—has, well, lost his stuff.

As I sink into my morning routine, a symphony of yelling, stomping, crying, and affirmations that the world is coming to an end shatters my concentration. His fleece jacket is missing! On top of that, my six-year-old daughter has a fever and is planning to stay home sick. With my wife out of commission, this is shaping up to be a challenging morning/day.

As I think about how ridiculous my son's reaction is to his missing jacket, I can feel my blood pressure rise a bit. I begin to realize there is no way of getting around addressing this issue. However, I am not going to address it now. He's a big boy and I have trained him how to handle these scenarios, so he'll figure it out, right? Wrong! I am loudly interrupted as my son barges through the door. I begin to consider the idea that the time has come to take care of this dire emergency.

However, since I am set on protecting my routine, I tell him to go look for the jacket himself. After ten more minutes of the symphony that only a nine-year-old in full-on tantrum mode can create, my procrastination gives way to action.

As I stand up to get out of my chair, a shadow I have named "Fireside" takes charge and I storm toward the door. My first instinct is to throw the door open, barge out, and in my best "mad dad" voice let him know how ridiculous this is. However, just as I arrive at the door, I am graced by a moment of clarity and I realize that Fireside was running the show. This piece of myself had served me very well on the playground when I was growing up, but when wielded against my son, it is nothing short of destructive.

Through this sudden shift of awareness, I gained a new perspective. I was forced to ask myself, "Are you wielding this powerful shadow with wisdom and control?" Now I stand behind a door with a choice. How do I choose to proceed?

In that moment, I made an intentional choice to approach my son with compassion rather than fire. I was able to open the door, give him a hug, and talk through this problem with him. He was able to calm down and take my message in. If I had leaned into my initial reaction and come running out the door yelling and screaming, we both would have missed this amazing opportunity to struggle and grow together. I am a better man for being challenged and being forced to look at myself in a moment of struggle, and he is a better person for learning how to utilize systems.

CHOOSING OUR PERSPECTIVE

Just like myself in this last story, there are pieces of yourself that you shove down and pretend don't exist. They rear their ugly head at the worst possible time and have the potential to send you into spirals of depression, anxiety, shame, doubt, fear, and anger. You can choose to ignore them, or you can chose to explore and reintegrate them. Through awareness, you will gain the opportunity to choose how you want to react, and that will make all the difference.

Remember that struggle is another word for opportunity. Just like with weight lifting, the opportunity for growth comes from the struggle. Struggle is a part of life. Whether it brings you to your knees or acts as the catalyst for growth, struggle and a subsequent change are inevitable. Perhaps it's time to accept that change is coming and lean into the ensuing struggle. Lean in and play with it. Stop learning the same lesson over and over and over. Internalize and leverage your struggle and move on to the next growth opportunity.

As we continue with this chapter, try to become aware of some of your patterns and keep some of your disowned qualities in the forefront of your mind. As your awareness grows, your roadblocks will begin to crumble as you shift your perspective. You will be given the gift of experiencing a new existence as you move forward and change the world with intention.

In the appendix, you can find a simplified (perhaps over-simplified) conceptualization of our potential roadblocks and the gifts we receive by leaning into the struggle of growth.

The reality is that we will never get to experience the gifts from the far right column without doing the work. We must play the game if we want the rewards. Notice that each column has a common theme. The second column, which is titled "Benefit of Avoiding the Struggle," is all about easy and comfortable. It's easy to sit on the sidelines and do nothing. We don't have to risk anything. That is why so many people stay in this column.

Column 3, which is titled "Drawbacks of Avoiding the Struggle," is all about stagnation. All actions have a consequence, and those consequences can be positive or negative. However, doing nothing provides its own set of consequences. The consequence of leaning into safety and security is that we stagnate. To clarify, I'm not promoting recklessness. I am promoting stretching. Get comfortable with being uncomfortable. The third column is all about confidence, fortitude, alignment, and bravery. When we play the game, we reap the rewards.

You don't have to take my word for any of this. Try it out for yourself. Push yourself to look at life with a new perspective and see what happens. To me, it's worth the gamble. How about you?

Take a moment to take stock of where you are in your life. Find the areas of this chart you are doing well on and the areas where you can improve. Then accept where you are and move forward with a rejuvenated perspective.

Be honest with yourself. Find an area that you feel you can grow and begin to create awareness around that part of your life. Remember that as our awareness grows (no matter how small), we begin to shape a vision for a better life and a better world. That is powerful.

MISTAKES MAKE US POWERFUL

Oftentimes our mistakes and failures are what created struggle in the first place. Maybe we forget to email someone or, worse yet, maybe we hit "reply all" instead of just "reply." Ouch! Just like with struggle, mistakes are great opportunities for growth. The sooner we accept that, the sooner we will develop an ability to lean into our mistakes with optimism. This is an act of self-love and an important step toward wholeness.

There are people who spend their entire life protecting their fragile ego and feel that admission of a mistake makes them weak. Once again, you can be right or you can be happy. Admitting and accepting your mistakes and then analyzing your failures will make you powerful and bring more contentment to your life. If you love the struggle, because you know great growth is around the corner, then what is there to despair?

I have talked a lot in this book about awareness and how we cannot have awareness without responsibility. If we are self-aware, we will naturally take an honest look at our mistakes and our failures. Eventually, honesty with ourselves becomes an intrinsic drive.

Conversely, when we choose to bury our head in the sand and blame others for our mistakes, we inadvertently miss the opportunity to make ourselves better. When we do this over and over again, we begin to feel like something is missing in our life. Eventually, this leads to feelings of inadequacy, emptiness, alienation, and depression. Accepting, owning, and taking responsibility for our mistakes may be tough and we may not desire the consequences, but ultimately, this responsibility makes us whole.

There is a question I often ask myself. This question helps me when I am feeling beaten down and defeated. It helps shift my perspective back toward a growth mindset.

Why was this mistake and struggle meant to happen?

If it was meant to happen, then I feel like the situation is a gift rather than a burden.

COMMITMENT AND FAITH

Given the fact that we are all going to make mistakes, and knowing this journey toward our highest self is hard, commitment and faith become essential. We have to discover what it is that we truly want and then we must dedicate ourselves to our desires. Without dedication, our desires are mere pipedreams.

What are you committed to? For real? Are you committed to saving money, or are you committed to hitting the drive-through at Starbucks every morning for your venti, caramel, mega-caf espresso?

At the end of the day, your life is the result of your commitments. You may say, "I'm not committed to being in a terrible relationship. I'm committed to finding the right person for me."

Yet, for some reason, these challenging relationships always seem to find you. If you truly are committed to finding the perfect relationship, you would not relive the same relationship over and over. Every relationship would be a building block for the next. Each relationship would be better and better, until you find the one. All your life choices have guided you to where you currently are, and they will continue to direct your life. Our choices are the result of our commitments, so it is imperative that we become crystal clear on our commitments.

My journey toward creating intentional commitments began when I started talking with others (others see your commitments so much more clearly) to learn more about myself. My first session with a therapist started with me saying, "Well, I get mad in traffic; I wonder what that's about." That ridiculous statement was my first topic in therapy. Was that my real issue? Definitely not.

From there, I learned about subconscious commitments I had set for myself throughout life. We all create stories about ourselves from the day we are born, and those stories create our commitments. As humans, we need to learn about, discuss, dissect, review, and understand our stories if we ever want to know what we are committed to. How can we change our commitments if we don't understand what they are or where they came from? That is where therapy and coaching is beyond powerful. If you are not talking with a trusted person about your stories, start now! It's time to understand your story so you can change it and make your story serve you.

Let's do a quick and simple exercise. Forget about what you

want to be committed to. Get out of your head for a moment and focus on what you have created in your life right now. Today. Right this moment. Forget about what you think you are committed to and just write down the results of your life right now. There may be results you are proud of and there may be results you wish were different. I'll say it again. Your results are the product of what you are committed to. Time to make a list. What are you committed to right now?

Here are the first five items on my list:

- Teaching my kids
- Raising the energy of the world by empowering and inspiring others to create their own uplifting legacy that propagates through generations
- Being overwhelmed
- Competition
- Strong relationships

That is just a snippet of my list. Yours may be 100 times longer. The important thing is to just keep asking yourself, "What do I have in my life currently?" Then go back through the list with an understanding that you can change your commitments at any time.

The next question to ask is, "What am I not committed to that I wish I were?" If you could create a list of all the things you wish you were more committed to, what does that list look like?

Here are the first five items on my list:

- Bravery
- Health
- Growth
- Financial freedom
- Stability

The items on your second list are perfectly achievable. The fact they are in list 2 just means that you are not committed to them right *now*. There's always room for improvement, but give yourself credit. You are successful, and you have room to grow. The story of our lives!

One other thing to consider is that these lists will change over time. I am writing my list before this book gets published so it will be different the next time you see me. It will forever grow and change, just like your list.

The second list underpins our goals. Behind all our goals (make more money, generate more business, get married to our soulmate, buy a Maserati, get a promotion, whatever), is a commitment. When we choose to commit to the items in the second list, all the other stuff will follow. Our commitment will drive us toward our goals.

As we become aware of our commitments and we shape new ones, we will inevitably find ourselves in times of fear, weakness, or doubt. This is where bravery comes into the picture. Remember that bravery is the act of intentionally moving forward in the face of fear or doubt. Now that we are consciously aware of our commitments, we can move forward with fortitude even though we experience fear and doubt.

There will come a time when we have set intentions, iden-
tified our commitments, and we feel aligned. Yet our circumstances seem to crush our spirit. That is where we must lean
into something called *faith*. This journey doesn't always follow
a straight path, so as we look to design our commitments,
we must have faith that everything will work out the way it is
supposed to.

Sometimes we begin to question whether we have made
the right choices, and we feel like we should give up. After all,
it would be much easier that way, remember. That's when faith
steps in. When we trust ourselves and the universe, then and only
then, can we find bravery in the face of fear and move forward.

GRATITUDE

Moving forward toward a better version of ourselves is no
easy task. Pieces of ourselves must take a back seat in order
for new pieces of us to start driving. That can be a tough pill
to swallow, but it is part of the natural progression of life and
growth. I have found that when I get to these crossroads and
I need something to propel me onward, that is when I tap into
gratitude. When I find gratitude for my struggles, I am able to
remind myself that a struggle is part of the process and the only
way I can grow. From this place I find resiliency.

Gratitude can instantly turn a burden into a gift. This is
why I incorporate gratitude practices into my day-to-day life.
Every night at dinner, my family and I go around the table and
we talk about one thing that went well in our day, one thing that
we could have done better, and one thing we are grateful for.

We also use this time to set an intention for the next day. A few nights ago, my daughter said, "I am grateful for my eyeballs! I couldn't see without them." I can honestly say I never planned to express my gratitude for my eyeballs at the dinner table, but her comment was a great reminder that we all have something to be grateful for.

How many of us take the time to stop and appreciate our ability to see, walk, talk, and be alive? Sometimes it takes the innocence of a child to help us realize what was right in front of us this whole time. We always have something to be grateful for, and the more we focus on it, the more fortitude and resiliency we find when it's time to summon bravery.

I have also found that finding gratitude right before I go to bed is powerful. Every night, I write down one thing that either went well that day or one thing I am grateful for. Not only do I write my gratitude on a Post-it note, but I take a moment and I feel my gratitude for that moment. I let it sink into my soul, and I experience it again. It is a great practice that allows me to remind myself of all the things I have to be grateful for every day. I now have a giant box full of Post-its, and when I need a quick smile or soul boost, I open the box and begin reading. I will save all these Post-its forever. They represent the good in my life, and they are a powerful proclamation of my thankfulness for the struggle.

Showing gratitude through a daily practice may seem trivial, but in the end, it is a proclamation. Even if we feel frustrated at the end of the day, taking a moment to be thankful is so powerful. It becomes a daily reminder that our struggle is our lifeblood. Our struggle leads to growth and brings us closer to our highest being. Without struggle, do we even have a purpose? That is why gratitude is so important.

Perhaps it's worth it to take a moment to write down a list of everything you are thankful for. Every person you are thankful for. Every opportunity you are thankful for. Every struggle you are thankful for. Here is my very abridged list, just to help get the juices flowing.

- I am thankful for my kids who have become my greatest teachers. Without them, I would be stuck in a consistent daily routine devoid of exceptional challenges. They have taught me how to play more, work less, and not take life too seriously.
- I am thankful for my amazing wife, Allison. She challenges me to be a better man and is a constant reminder of my true potential.
- I am thankful for America, my homeland.
- I am thankful for my mom, raising three kids, going to school, working, and showing all her love. She has had a profound impact on my life.
- I am thankful for my dad and my stepmom, Debbie. Their strength has taught me to stand up for myself while maintaining a high level of integrity.
- I am thankful for some of the most loyal and supportive friends anyone could ever ask for.
- I am thankful for a safe home.
- I am thankful for my health, my body, my eyeballs, and

simply being alive.

- I am thankful for my in-laws. Their faith in us has created great opportunities, and I am forever grateful for the risks they have taken in me.
- I am thankful for all life's struggles and lessons. Without them, I would be bored out of my mind.
- I am thankful for a desire to grow.

Most of all, I am thankful for the joy that I have in my life. In the end, that is all I need and want. A massive thank you to all of you who have been by my side and supported me along my journey to find love, passion, playfulness, power, perspective, and joy. You are my angels.

I believe that when we are unhappy, it's because we aren't whole. Gratitude reminds us that we have been given so much, and we have so much to give. As we find gratitude in our life, we find wholeness. When we have gratitude, anything is possible, because we realize we already have and are everything we need or want.

CHAPTER 9

INTENTION

"Nothing can stop the man with the right mental attitude from achieving his goal; nothing on earth can help the man with the wrong mental attitude."

—Thomas Jefferson

THE PURPOSE OF THE FIRST SECTION in this chapter is to briefly describe the subtle yet very important difference between intentions, goals, and tasks. It can be a tough distinction to qualify, but I believe it is important to understand the difference. As we move through this chapter, I would like to keep our focus on intention-setting rather than goal-setting, because our intentions carry more power as we look to create the life we desire.

An intention has an intrinsic energy that derives from our desires. So, an intention is similar to a desire, but it's really more like a desire in action. An intention directs our energy and our thoughts in a way that ultimately dictates goals and tasks.

Goals are more of a means to an end. They are a product of our intention. We create goals as a way to fulfill our intention.

It's fairly common for my kids to set intentions around the dinner table that are really more like goals. They will say things like, "My intention is to do the dishes tomorrow." That is a goal. A true intention might sound more like, "My intention is to be in integrity with my word. I give my word to do the dishes tomorrow."

In the example, the intention is to "be in integrity with our word." This intention is driven by an intrinsic desire and, therefore, has a deeper meaning to it. So, in the end, our intention to keep our word will drive us toward the attainment of our goal. This is where the power of intention really comes into to play. More on that later.

Tasks are pretty straightforward. Once we have an intention and we have set some goals, we can assign tasks that will actually get us to the finish line. These are the activities we must do in order to remain in integrity with our intention and to accomplish our goal.

So, to bring it all together using this example, our intention is to be in integrity with our word. Our goal is to get the dishes done. Our task is to actually, physically, do the dishes.

So why does any of this matter? Why do we need to focus on intention-setting rather than goal-setting? In the end, intentions create action toward the attainment of our goals. If we focus only on goals, we may run out of steam before we ever complete all our tasks. Our intentions are tied to our intrinsic desires, so they drive us forward through adversity.

OUR WHY

In a perfect world, having an intention would be all it takes to attain our goals. Unfortunately, in the real world, we may occasionally have great intentions and still fall short of meeting our goals. I believe the saying is "The road to hell is paved with good intentions." When this happens, what do we do about it?

Typically, when we set an intention and we still fall short of achieving our goals, it's because we were not clear about *why* we have set that intention in the first place. Our why(s) fortify and reinforce our intention, which ultimately fuels our desire and keeps our drive strong even in times of struggle and doubt. When we run into roadblocks or challenges, we need to know why we have set our intention so we can move forward with fortitude.

It's also worth noting that we can have multiple reasons why we have an intention. We don't have to always boil it down to one why. For example, we may have an intention to have our body operate at its peak performance, because we want to look good, feel good, and fit into our swimsuit before pool season. No matter the reason, defining our why(s) develops fortitude within our intention. Now that we know what we want and why we want it, we are much more likely to hit the pool with confidence!

POWER OF INTENTIONS

Over the years, I have begun to realize how powerful intentions are, mainly because our intentions tend to be the things in our life we place the most focus on. Not only that, but what we focus on *is* our reality. Therefore, it would make sense that if our intentions create focal points in our life, then our intentions create our reality. It's not magic or some secret.

For example, we can chose to focus on not being poor or we can choose to focus on being wealthy. Similarly, we can focus on not getting into another bad relationship or we can focus on the perfect relationship. The respective intentions in each scenario have a similar end game in mind. We want more money and we want a better relationship. OK, so what's the difference? The difference is that one intention is focused on the avoidance of a negative outcome and the other is focused on the attainment of a positive outcome. The bittersweet reality is that no matter what you focus on, you're right!

The reason intentions work is because our intentions become a focal point in our mind. Our brain naturally seeks out what we focus on. If we focus on being rich, then when financially beneficial opportunities arise, we are hyperaware of the opportunity, and we strike. When we are focused on not being poor, we are hyper-aware of keeping the $100 in our pocket, while being completely unaware of the potential profit we could have made by investing that same $100. Stepping over quarters to pick up pennies. So, if our focus is not to be poor, we may be very astute at sniffing out every scam and every possible way someone can take advantage of us. We may see tremendous opportunities as we clip coupons for the grocery store, but we miss every opportunity to become wealthy. In both scenarios, our intentions are working perfectly! One intention creates money, and one creates conservation of money. The original goal was very similar, but the outcomes are very different, and aligned with the intention in both cases

Similarly, if we focus on not being in a bad relationship, our focus is on bad relationships and we will see only bad relationships. We see the couple walking down our street, not talking and standing three feet apart. We notice the couple sitting at the dinner table next to us not talking because their heads are buried in their phones. There are bad relationships everywhere, and it's apparent that good relationships are actually just a show. If we focus on fantastic relationships, we see examples of great relationships everywhere. We notice an old couple walking down the street holding hands. We notice a couple having a nice conversation at the dinner table next to us. Our reality is that great relationships are everywhere. It's only a matter of time before we find our perfect relationship. With this mindset, we are more likely to internalize and learn about great relationships through observation. We may even seek out a counselor or teacher to move us along toward finding the perfect someone.

Our intentions drive our actions. What we focus on, we find.

It is important to note that there are always positive and negative outcomes for pursuing our intentions, so we have to become very conscious when we set and analyze them. If we focus on being rich, we will make more money. It will happen.

We may be so successful that we miss a great sale on a new BBQ grill because our focus is on making enough money to buy three full-price BBQ grills rather than buying one on sale. However, that ability to make money doesn't mean we are automatically happy. We may miss opportunities to play with our kids, because that's not our focus. There are tradeoffs for all our intentions. We must become very aware of where we choose to place our focus.

We also need to get really clear on how our intention is worded or constructed. Remember if we set an avoidance intention, the thing we are trying to avoid is our focal point, so guess what we bring into our life? Our focus needs to be on what we want to bring into our life.

This chapter is about creating new intentions through awareness so we regain control over our future. We don't have to be aware of our intentions for them to control our life. We are subconsciously focused on all kinds of stuff all the time. My kids are nine and six so it may not come as a surprise that they are not the best at remembering their intention. I probably forget mine 10 percent of the time too. However, there have been countless instances when the kids set their intention one evening and when we review the next day, they say, "I can't remember what my intention was." Then my wife and I remind them what it was. They think about it and say, "Oh, right! Yes, I did meet my intention." They met their intention even though they weren't consciously focused on it, because by simply internalizing their thought the night before, they created a focal point in their mind.

I am a firm believer in setting daily intentions. By sitting around the dinner table and discussing tomorrow's intentions, we open up our mind to creating a better life every day. With that said, just mentioning an intention will only go so far. If we really want our intentions to sink in, then we need to *feel* them. At our house, after everyone has shared our intention, we go back through and everyone restates their intention, while they close their eyes and imagine meeting it. I know you are now picturing me and my family sitting around the table with our eyes closed. It's kind of hilarious, and I am glad no one films it. I'll tell you this, though. Although we may look like a bunch of crazy people, it works!

I'd like to take it one step further. My kids are not quite there yet, but they will get there. I have a morning routine when I avoid looking at my phone first thing in the morning. I sit in bed right after I wake up, and I think about what my intention is for the day. I visualize me meeting my intention. Typically, my intention is centered around who I want to be that day or how I want to show up in the world. This practice reinforces my intention from the night before and focuses my brain on what I want out of this day. That way, even if I go on autopilot, I have a powerful subconscious focal point all day that drives me forward.

If you don't have a practice like this, I would highly recommend that you give it a shot. Outside of looking a little crazy, what do you have to lose? Conversely, what do you have to gain? At the very least, it will force the TV off and allow everyone time to connect. It can bring a family together, and if you are alone, it gives you time to focus on yourself for a few minutes a day. This practice gets everyone thinking about his or her daily intentions.

Why did I decide to write an entire chapter that focuses on intention rather than goals? It's simple really. A goal without an intention is like a train with no track. It may be worth something, but it sure as hell isn't serving its intended purpose! The intention is what drives us forward and creates the impetus for change. So let's do this thing! Let's set some intentions!

FINDING YOUR INTENTIONAL INTENTIONS

Below is a series of questions that will help get the juices flowing. I recommend getting out a piece of paper and physically writing down the answers to these questions. As you write, new ideas will flow. Don't stop. Write down all the stuff that seems to make no sense. It may not make sense now, and it may never make sense, but many times our seemingly ridiculous answers actually hold our greatest wisdom. Don't be shy. No one else will read this unless you want them to. Write it *all* down!

1. What kind of person do you want to be today?
2. How do you want to show up in the world today?
3. What you commit to is what actually shows up in your world. What are you committed to today? Yummy food, chilling, working out, spending time with family or friends, looking good for others, distraction, etc.?
4. How are those commitments serving you in a positive way? Make you happy, comfortable, easy, etc.?

5. How are those commitments serving you in a destructive way? Unfulfilling, unhealthy, anxious, etc.?

6. How do you want to show up in the world in the long term? Powerful, sympathetic, energetic, relaxed, peaceful, happy, content, etc.? Another way to look at this question is how do you want other people to experience you? Or, if you died today, what would you hope everyone says about you during your eulogy? That question may be a bit morbid, but for me it really helped bring the essence of who I want to be to the surface.

7. Who do you want to be in the long term? How do you want to influence the world?

8. How do you want to feel when you achieve or while working toward achieving your goals? Challenged, happy, content, fulfilled, etc.?

The answers to these questions will become your basis for your intentions. Some people will wrap these questions up in five minutes, and others may take six months. You may have all the answers right at your fingertips, and you may be drawing a complete blank. No matter how long it took you to finish these questions, I recommend revisiting and recreating this list regularly. As you go on your journey, the answers will change. The more aware you are about who you want to be, the more you will become that person. Remember, intention is really just a focal point, so the more you focus on this stuff, the more your intention will guide you toward the you that you want to be.

I mentioned that for some, this practice may seem easy and

for others it may be very difficult. Wherever you are … that's perfect. Whether you are stuck or just plowing through this exercise, here are a few tips I have found to be useful to help encourage the creation of your list.

1. Meditate. I will go over this more below, but for now, all I can say is that meditation is as close to magic as we will ever come.
2. Get help. Talk with people. Perhaps find a few trusted people (family, friends, coach, counselor) who you can share this list with. It may be uncomfortable, but you will get amazing feedback. You must find bravery. You must be vulnerable. You must risk. Your bravery will be rewarded. Even if the person you share with laughs in your face, you will gain some form of wisdom from that exercise. Get brave and share part of you with the world, and then open yourself up to feedback. I promise you will thank yourself one day!
3. Review and continue your practice regularly. Focus on who you want to be and continue to grow/solidify your intentions as much as possible.

After all that, what are your intentions? What are the top three things you want to work on to make yourself better?

I know it's tough, but after leaning into this exercise, your life will never be the same. Take a risk. You have nothing to lose. Even if this is all just a giant prank and my goal is to make you look silly, by doing this exercise, you have proven your willingness to change. Through your willingness to change, you have stepped into a place of open-mindedness, risk, struggle, acceptance, and faith. Even if I am just screwing with you, the joke is on me, because when you step into that kind of power, there is no downside. You have just made yourself and the world better, and that is a fact. Great work! Keep it up.

MEDITATION

Meditation may still seem a little "woo-woo," but there are more books being written about it, more content showing up on the internet, and the science is beginning to catch up with the practice. It seems to me that meditation is becoming more and more acceptable in America. One of the best tools I have ever found to bring me to the present and bring awareness is meditation. The list of benefits goes on and on, but here is a list of some of the most common benefits:

- Reduces stress
- Opens up conduits for creativity
- Reduces anxiety
- Promotes emotional health
- Enhances self-awareness
- Lengthens attention span
- Calms nerves
- Helps ground us
- Helps develop a connection to the rest of the world/ universe
- Can help fight addictions

- Improves sleep
- Can decrease blood pressure
- Can help fight depression
- Increases focus
- Improves mood
- Improves and strengthens resolve and commitments
- Promotes self-compassion
- Increases work productivity
- Strengthens relationships

The only negatives I can come up with for meditation is that it takes time, dedication, intention, and an open mind. That may be hard to do at first, but obviously, the benefits greatly outweigh the negatives.

So, how does it work? Let me start by saying that you can't mess this up. When I started my meditation practice, I had no idea what I was doing. However, I still reaped many benefits. As you practice, the benefits may increase, but a little mediation is better than none.

My first attempts at meditation came when I was first embarking on this self-exploration journey. I tried meditation only when I was super stressed out. It was not a daily practice at that time. I would simply lie down in my bed, turn on soft music, close my eyes, focus on my breathing, and try to clear my mind. I fell asleep nearly every time. Although falling asleep was not my intended purpose, there were many benefits to starting out this way. First of all, there was time before and after I fell asleep when I was able to get out of my own way (even if it was for only a minute or two). Additionally, when I did fall asleep, my mind was in a state of relaxation, and sometimes sleeping was exactly what I needed. Finally, the combination of meditating before I fell asleep opened a door in my mind. Very frequently, I would have these moments of clarity as I regained consciousness. Ideas would pop into my mind, and I would notice internal transformations. In an instant, my world would change, my energy would shift, and I was no longer the same person.

There are many people out there who might say I was "doing it wrong," and that doesn't bother me one bit. There is no right or wrong! All I know is that I was trying, and I gained a great deal from those meditations.

Over time, I realized that if I sat cross-legged (I had to use blocks under my legs at first) I was able to stay awake, and that created a whole different experience. Once again, not right or wrong, but definitely different. I started this sitting practice with a five- to ten-minute meditation a few times a week. Eventually, I began to incorporate yoga into my practice as well. Now I meditate nearly every day, sometimes for five minutes and sometimes for thirty. It just depends on my mood and where I am that day.

I want to make it very clear that every practice is different. Every time you sit down to meditate, it is a unique experience. Keep an open mind when meditating, especially if you are new to it.

What's the best way to get started? That is a valid question. There are countless books and websites dedicated to meditation. Simply Google meditation or mindfulness, and you will have all the ammo you need to get started. The website and app, Headspace, has a ton of guided meditations. I used Headspace when I started my practice, and it is a great place to begin. YouTube also has some fantastic guided meditations. Eventually I moved away from guided meditations, because I enjoy just sitting with my own thoughts, but, once again, these are great places to start.

You don't have to take my word for it. Just try it. Five minutes to start is fine. You don't have to sit under the Bodhi tree until you reach enlightenment. Just start your practice, get still, relax, and enjoy.

If you are truly are serious about bringing change into your life, meditation *must* become part of your daily routine. It's one of those things I can't explain. You must experience it, but I promise that once you do, you will understand what I am talking about.

Here are a few tips that have helped me as I developed my practice:

1. Start where you start, and don't judge yourself. Don't compare yourself to anyone else. This is *your* sacred practice! As a practice and a journey, it takes time to learn. If you can do thirty minutes every day, great. If you can do only thirty seconds every week, great. Just like with running, as you practice you will be able to go longer.

2. If you're a first-timer, try lying down or sitting in a comfortable chair. Starting in a comfortable place will make the transition more fun.

3. Some people like silence when they meditate, and some people like guided meditations. I like unguided meditations with light music playing in the background. There is no right way. Play with it to find your preference.

4. Focus on your breath. There is a reason behind this. It takes your mind off of your conscious brain, and places it on a simple task. You don't have to change your breathing, but just notice it and flow with it. Your mind will naturally wander when meditating. Many call this "monkey mind." Accept monkey mind, love it for what it is, and simply come back to your breath when you notice your mind drifting. I can promise you will have to do this over and over and over, so get used to it.

5. Close your eyes and focus on your third eye. Similar to the previous item, this will allow you to shift your focus onto something other than your conscious thoughts. I am sure there is more to this one than I know about, but all I know is that it helps ground and shift my focus.

6. Try to relax your body. Many times, when I first begin my practice, I notice that I am holding tension everywhere. Sometimes in my shoulders, sometimes in my neck, sometimes in my legs, and sometimes in my face. Do a quick body scan, find your tension, and do what you can to relax those areas. Just like all of this, it takes practice. But here's the great news: I have found that getting regular massages helps my muscles learn to

relax when I want them to. Yes, that's right. I just told you that if you want to change the world, you have to get more massages. You're welcome!

7. Try different mudras, more commonly known as hand positionings. It's crazy how different the energy can be with different mudras. Google's got your back on this one.

8. Move your body daily. I started meditating either before or after a yoga practice. The timing of my meditation creates very different feelings. The physical movement combined with a meditation is powerful. Our bodies want to move. So even if it's a stretching routine, try to incorporate some movement into your practice. It may even make you more likely to continue.

9. Try it in nature. Sitting on the bare ground while meditating can be very powerful.

10. Set an intention at the beginning, and then let it go. The universe will speak to you. You don't have to find the answers with your conscious brain. You just have to let go of what you think you know and then listen. The first time this happened to me, I was sold, and I have never looked back. Nearly all my major revelations in my recent life have come through a meditation practice. That includes the outline for this entire book. I had no idea I was going to write this book until I knew I was going to write this book. I came out of a meditation one day, and in an instant, the entire outline popped into my head. I got up and wrote my rough outline in

about twenty minutes. In an unexpected moment of inspiration, I knew exactly what to do. World changed in a literal moment.

11. Be patient. Just like with anything, you have to practice to see results, and the results make it all worthwhile. I am so much more calm now that I have a daily meditation practice. By quieting my mind on a daily basis, I find myself more even-keeled throughout the day. It's almost as if my mind knows how to take a step back and relax during challenging times. Don't get me wrong; I still experience emotions like anger and frustration, and I have my moments where I lose it, but the practice of meditating absolutely helps temper my emotions and keeps me thinking more clearly and calmly.

12. Accept that you will have days that are harder than others to get into the zone. That's OK. Sometimes your mind will slip right into your practice, and sometimes your mind will be all over the place. Meditation is about acceptance. Don't judge yourself. Just relax. Through the act of trying, you are doing it right. It's that simple.

I've included a guided meditation for setting intentions in the appendix. Play with it and have fun. This is a practice. Make the practice your playground. The more you lighten up and just try, the more fun you will have and the more success you will see. What do you have to lose?

SETTING YOUR NEW EMPOWERING INTENTIONS

Intentions start within you. You already have all the answers you will ever need right within yourself. A meditation practice is meant to help you communicate with the universe and with your highest being in order to bring out the answers you already have within you.

What is your intention? What is your driving force? What is going to keep you moving forward through adversity? Remember that we have many intentions in our life. Some of them are big and some of them are small, but the relationship we have with one intention is the same relationship we have with all our intentions. How we do one thing is how we do all things. As you move into the process of creating your own inspiring story, take stock of your current intentions and your relationship with them.

This chapter is designed to get you to start thinking about who you want to be and how you want to show up in your world. It's intended to get you to find the driving force behind all your goals. You may not get all the answers you want after going through this process the first time, and that is OK. Keep working on yourself and keep the curiosity alive. The simple act of trying is all you need to change yourself and to change the world.

CHAPTER 10

CREATE YOUR INSPIRING STORY

*"To be ordinary is not a choice: It is the usual
freedom of men [and women] without [their]
vision."*

—Thomas Merton

NOW THAT WE HAVE STARTED the work (remember,
this is lifelong work) on creating our intentions, we can start the
process of goal-setting.

As I mentioned before, we can set countless goals around
one intention, because our goals are products of our intention.
The more we focus on our intention, the more our goals and
tasks will naturally support our intention and the more fulfilled

we become. At this point, I challenge you to take a risk. Step out of your comfort zone and learn something new about yourself. Your world will never be the same.

VISION

Fame is an odd thing. The other day, my son and I were on a bike ride. As we passed by a guy walking his dog, my son acknowledged this person by saying "Hi" as he rode past. When we got about a hundred yards away, I stopped and turned to my son and asked, "Do you know who that was?"

"No, who was it?"

"That was Michael Malone, the coach for the Nuggets."

"What?!" he exclaimed. "That was the Nuggets head coach?" He looked back in awe.

"I can't believe I just saw him! That is so cool!"

In one moment, that was just a guy. In the next moment he was Michael Malone. It's almost like he was a different person. I couldn't help but be reminded of the undeniable fact that fame is a complete illusion. A person is famous and exceptional only if we recognize that the person is famous and exceptional. If we don't know who they are, they are just another random person. This speaks to the idea that we are all amazing humans who have something to give to this world.

A few years ago, I came up with a quote that exemplifies this concept very well: "I already am famous. I am famous to everyone who already knows who I am."

Here's the point. Celebrities are just regular people, and they are inherently the same as you and me. However, one of the biggest differences between "ordinary" people and people who have made great accomplishments is *vision*.

Bring to mind three people who you think have great vision. They can be living or dead. Obviously, these answers are going to vary, but I can guarantee that most, if not all three people who popped into your mind are/were famous people. People like Steve Jobs, George Washington, or Mark Cuban. Those are just a few examples, but in the end, when most people think about others who have vision, they tend to think about fairly accomplished individuals.

Because they are so accomplished, it is very common for us to look at these people as superhuman, like they are inherently different from us. Perhaps they seem to be capable of things that are so outside the realm of possibility for us, that, in a way, we dehumanize them. Many people call this "putting them on a pedestal."

We forget they are just like me and you. Fame becomes a barrier between them and us, and we forget they are, in fact, human. We forget they have emotions, struggles, deficiencies, and strengths, just like me and just like you. Our conscious brain knows all this, but our emotional being may not fully comprehend those facts. Their accomplishments may be very impressive, and I am not here to diminish what any celebrity or major world changer has done. What I am trying to say is that, on a fundamental level, they are the same as us, but with one notable difference. Vision!

You may be saying there are plenty of people out there who fell ass-end into money or fame, and I agree. But, for the sake of this book, I am simply using accomplished people as an example of what happens when we have vision. There are plenty of people out there who don't have vision, and yet they seem to have it all. However, fame isn't the end-all, be-all. They may seem to have it all, and they may have fame or money, but without a vision, all they have is fame and fortune. Until they create a vision for themselves, they are destined to walk through life with no real purpose and they will ultimately destroy themselves from the inside out. This is a universal truth! Without something to work toward, our soul begins to wither and die.

Top-tier inventors, athletes, professionals, coaches, actors, CEOs, singers, and presidents are just like you and me, but they also have a clear vision about what they want to create. At some point, they clearly defined what they want out of life, and then they went after that vision with a passion that couldn't be denied. They are not superhuman. They are just very clear on what they want.

Our greatness begins with vision. Our greatness may involve fame and fortune, our greatness may involve shifting the energy of the entire world, or our vision may be to influence our small circle in a positive way. The actual composition of our vision is irrelevant. The beautiful part is that we get to choose our own vision, and we get to choose how big or how small we want to play. Ultimately, having a vision is all that really matters.

PREPARE YOURSELF TO
CREATE YOUR VISION

If you ask a thousand artists how they get into a place of inspiration, you will probably get a thousand different answers. I have a routine I use to prepare myself to envision a better future. I recommend you create your own routine. I will share some strategies that have worked for me, but that doesn't mean you need to do it the same way.

A routine can be a very personal thing. Perhaps you can take these ideas and use them as a starter kit to help you develop your personalized strategy. Play around with your strategy, and try new things. Remember that the world is our playground if we choose to accept it as such. Like everything in this book, have fun with your process. Finding a routine, defining vision, and tapping into our inspiration can be work, but it can also be a lot of fun. Once we find inspiration, it begins to feel more like playing than working. Inspiration has a little habit of putting the fun back into everything we do. Lean into your inspiration, and find your joy again. Below are a few strategies that have helped me prepare myself to find inspiration and create my vision.

Daily movement. Have you ever had a workout that was so intense that when you finished, you were exhausted, but felt amazing at the same time? Those are juicy moments for inspiration. In these moments, your body and mind are too tired to keep walls up. Therefore, your soul and intuition get to steer the ship for a few minutes.

Yoga is a fantastic way to move daily. I can do a practice in as little as fifteen minutes, and I don't even have to leave my house. That's not even the best part. For me, the best part about yoga is the powerful effect it has on my mood. The movement, the flow, the meditation, and the shift of focus break up the programs I'm running and get me back on track. It is amazing. If you are looking for a good place to start, check out "Yoga with Adrian" on YouTube. She provides tons of free yoga videos. Check her out, and do a thirty-day challenge and see how you feel.

Meditation. I have already covered this topic quite a bit, so I'll leave you with this one last thought. Shutting off your conscious mind opens the doorway to the superconscious. It creates a conduit for ideas to flow to you and through you. You already have all the answers you need, right within yourself.

Slow down and find time to think. Take some stuff off your plate and chill. In order to find inspiration, it is required to have time to think. We can think in the car or at home. It doesn't matter when or where, but if you want to be inspired to find your vision, you must intentionally find time in your schedule to think, ponder, philosophize, daydream, and expand.

Talk openly with other people. The more we talk with other people while keeping an open mind, the more we learn. Sometimes it's great to talk with people we resonate with, and sometimes it's great to talk with people who may think we are crazy. If we keep an open mind while having these conversations, we will *always* learn. Everyone has something to teach us.

Talk through ideas with coaches and counselors. These are people paid to make our life more challenging. If we accept that other people can provide solid feedback and lean into the idea that we are completely full of it, then coaches and counselors can help us get to the next stage very quickly.

Write. Just put your ideas down on paper. You matter, and so do your ideas. You may even surprise yourself with your own wisdom from time to time. You never know whose life you might change with those words one day.

Routine. A routine simplifies our lives by eliminating the distraction of continuous decision-making. When we have a routine, we wake up and know exactly what to do and where to put our focus and energy. After work, we know what to do and where to put our focus and energy. Simply put, a routine makes it easier to find inspiration by opening up more energy to focus on ideation rather than on what to do after lunch.

Practice. It takes time, dedication, and intention to make tasks into habits. Commit to the process of practice, and don't beat yourself up when you slip. Part of practice is learning, and part of learning is failure. This is a lifelong process. We are always practicing, failing, trying again, and learning.

Have fun with it. I've said it before, and I will say it again … and again … and again. Have fun with it! Find the humor and the fun while learning. This work can become a drag if we take it too seriously. Just try to be better every day, and smile. When we find the fun in the struggle, we can't lose. Say *F-it*. Find some hilarious, outrageous, and fantastic ideas that change the world, and run with them!

As you play with these ideas, and as you figure out what works for you, you will find more and more inspiration in your life. Inspiration is all around us. We just have to tap into it. Keep practicing, and good things will happen.

CREATE YOUR VISION

Time to create your own empowering vision, so you can "ball out" like all your heroes and idols. I find that visualization is key to creating a vision.

We are going to take a short journey in our mind. Creating vision is much easier when we give ourselves some time to quietly sit without distractions and with an open mind. This is important, so give yourself permission to be here and be present as we take this journey.

Close your eyes for a moment. Take a few deep breaths, and listen to the sound of your breathing. Relax your shoulders and sit quietly. Focus on your breath, and clear your mind of random thoughts. As you take your next breath in, ask the question, "What is my vision?" Trust whatever pops into your mind, and don't judge it.

Bring that vision to the forefront of your consciousness, and sit with it for a few breaths. Now let that thought disappear, and refocus your energy on your breath. Acknowledge any random thoughts that pop into your mind and then let them pass on by. Focus on your breathing. Notice where you are holding tension, and relax those muscles. As ideas pop up, acknowledge them and allow them to pass as you focus on your breath.

Once you have found stillness, imagine you're standing in a field at the edge of a lush forest. As you enter the forest, you feel the cool, damp air on your skin, and you can actually smell the moisture in the air as it combines with the aroma of blossoming flowers. The canopy of trees above your head nearly blocks out the sun; yet you are still warm and you feel totally at peace. After a short walk, you come to one tree that stands out for some reason. You can't put your finger on it. You walk over to this tree and as you look down at the base, you notice a shiny object lying in the tall grass. You're not quite sure what it is, but it is very beautiful. As you reach down pick it up, you realize it is a genie lamp. After taking in the beauty of the magic lamp, your curiosity gets the best of you and you give it a rub.

To your astonishment, a genie pops out in a wisp of smoke, and as he towers overhead, he looks right at you and in a warm voice he says, "Your wish is my command." He continues, "You don't need to ask or speak your wish. Simply imagine everything you want out of life, and I will make it happen in an instant. Anything is possible. How may I serve you and make your perfect life a reality?"

You are taken aback by this opportunity. Rather than the standard three wishes, this genie has just promised to give you *everything* you have ever wanted. All you have to do is imagine your perfect life, and it will manifest itself instantly.

Sit with your thoughts for a moment. What are you imagining? You don't have to define any of these thoughts in words. Just feel what this perfect life is like. Your perfect life is just a few thoughts away. Are you rich? Are you famous? Do you simplify your life? Do you still work, or do you play all day? Who are you with? What does your daily routine look like? How are you influencing the people around you? How are you influencing the world? What does this perfect life look like, and what does it feel like?

Take a few breaths and stay in this place. Feel the ultimate vision for your life and breathe it in. Feel it fully, and become one with this perfect existence. Continue to breathe.

As the vision of your perfect life takes shape, the genie looks down at you and says, "Your wish is my command." He nods his head and disappears back into the bottle. Whatever you envisioned is now a reality.

As the genie disappears, you set the lamp back down behind the tree. Now you know exactly where this tree is, and you are comforted by the fact that you can come back to this tree and summon the genie anytime you want. He will always be here to grant you any wish you want. But for now, it's time to leave the forest.

You turn around and head back down the path. Before you reach the edge of the forest, you turn around and take a moment to show gratitude for the forest, for the genie, and most importantly, for yourself.

As you exit the forest, begin to bring your attention back to your physical body. Bring some movement back into your fingers. As your attention comes back to the room you sit in, slowly open your eyes.

Grab a piece of paper and take a few notes. They don't have to make any sense. Write something down so you can refer back to it in the future. What did your vision look like? Was it a vision of a more powerful and fulfilled you, or did your thoughts digress into excuses and negative thoughts? Did your vision make you tear up as you realized what is possible for your life, or did your vision make you tear up as you realize how far away you are from the life you want? Did your vision inspire you to take action and create a new drive within yourself, or did it make you feel daunted and unmotivated?

As we move forward, remember that we reap what we sow. If we sow seeds of victimhood, anger, and blame, we reap that harvest. If we sow the seeds of intention, power, vision, and prosperity, we reap that harvest. Good thoughts, bad thoughts—no matter what your vision consists of, the genie will give that to you. So it goes the entirety of your life. We all have a vision. As we hold these images and ideas in our mind (good or bad), the "genie" gives us exactly what we envision.

Our ego always wants to be right. Therefore, we seek out and find evidence for what we already believe to be true. We create our own reality, every day. What you focus on... *is.*

You may not have known it, but the genie has been working for you your entire life. You now have the power and the tools to create a vision that feeds your soul. Your wish is your genie's command, always and forever.

We all want to believe that our life happens to us so we can dodge responsibility, but believe it or not, you have the ability to visualize and create your most powerful self. The time has come for you to create a vision that truly serves and promotes your highest self and highest purpose.

As I mentioned, you can visit your genie in your forest any time and create/alter your life vision. As you become more aware of your vision, you will begin to see things shift in your life. Eventually, your vision will become reality. Then you get to create an even bigger and more powerful vision. Dedicating yourself to creating a conscious vision is the first step in changing the world with intention.

Now take the image of the vision you saw in the forest and put words to it. Try to boil it down to a few sentences if you can. By keeping your experience short and succinct, it's easier to focus on during your day-to-day life. This process may take a lot of time and focus on the front end. It's possible you didn't even see a vision as we went through the vision process with the genie. That is OK. As I said, you can go back to that forest anytime. That is your forest and your genie. My only challenge to you is to do something—anything—and don't give up.

This is an important step to leading a life of intention. Don't sell yourself short and run away from the struggle. Lean into the struggle as you go through this process, and stick with it until you have a vision that empowers you.

My vision is to raise the energy of the world by empowering and inspiring others to create their own legacy that propagates through generations. There are many goals and objectives that feed into that vision. It is not a finite goal. It is an infinite journey that has no real end. This is a vision I have created for myself and for the world, and it is a vision I can fall back on in times of struggle and confusion. My vision is bigger than I am, and because it is based on making the world a better place, I find my vision empowering. The thing I love most about my vision is that I can't fail. Through the simple act of trying to make the world a better place, I have already succeeded.

Your vision can be just as powerful, but it takes intention. You may already have your vision. You may discover your vision tomorrow, or you may have to work to discover your vision for many years to come. No matter where you are, I challenge you to keep digging. Find something that inspires you to be the best version of yourself. And remember the simple act of trying means you have already succeeded.

FINDING INSPIRATION FOR VISION

Finding inspiration can be challenging sometimes, especially if we are stressed, overworked, discouraged, or just plain tired. The key to developing the life you desire, and the key to changing the world with intention, is a commitment to always trying. Inspiration tends to come in singular moments, and we never know when it will strike. By staying open to the process and staying committed to trying, inspiration is always right around the corner.

It can be scary to challenge our own status quo, but the gifts that come from this practice greatly outweigh the pain of doing nothing. Bravery arises when we know we need to do something, we know it will be hard, we know it is risky, and yet, we consciously move forward even in the face of fear. It's scary, but the fact remains, we can live in fear or we can live in our vision.

In the next few pages, I am going to give some strategies that I have used to help me find inspiration, but these are not the end-all and be-all. These are strategies that have worked for me, so perhaps they will help you as well. Take them for what they are and apply them as you see fit. This is your journey. Play, have fun, and change the world.

CHANGE IS PART OF THE PROCESS

I fully understand how hard it can be to find an authentically inspired vision. There are so many programs and roadblocks that create challenges to really tapping into our vision. It's kind of odd, really. It seems like we should be able to figure out our idealistic vision for our life with very little work, but the reality is that we often seem to get in our own way. Perhaps this happens because, at some point, we realize what we have to give up in order to own our vision. Perhaps this is because, at some point, we realize what is required of ourselves in order to go after it. Perhaps this is because we have simply drifted so far away from our true calling that we can't even seem to recognize what we want out of life anymore.

Like so many things in life, the first step to finding inspiration is to open up to acceptance. Once you embark on this journey of self-discovery, and once you commit to something greater than yourself, what once was will no longer be. There is a point of no return. Through an acceptance that a part of us must die or transform in order for a new part of us to be born, we liberate ourselves from our old patterns and excuses.

The first step in finding inspiration is acknowledging and accepting the truth. It's time for a change, and we can always do it better.

BE IDEALISTIC

How many visionaries play it safe? I would say not very many, if any. The noun *visionary*, in and of itself, represents someone who visualizes something that has not previously been created. Therefore, a visionary is idealistic. A visionary recognizes the discrepancy between where we are and where we are going. A visionary takes stock of current circumstances and then looks forward with limitless imagination.

When we sink into the idea that we change the world (which can be challenging to accept), we create the opportunity to think big and to think creatively. As you create a vision for your life, get idealistic. Get rid of the boundaries and just ideate. Write down all the ridiculous things you could imagine if your genie was sitting in front of you. Remember,

**this is your vision, and no one can tell
you that you're wrong.**

Embrace your creativity and get idealistic. In a perfect world, what would you be doing? Imagine how you feel while doing these amazing things, and internalize what it would feel like. That can be your reality! You can make that happen, but you won't make it happen until you visualize it.

Vision + intention = success. Success is not based on results. Success is based on your ability to create a vision and then intentionally strive toward that vision. If you are truly chasing your vision, you have already succeeded. Results are the fruit of the aforementioned work.

It all starts with a big vision. Get idealistic. Go big or go home!

INSPIRATIONAL IMMERSION

Maybe there is a person in your life who inspires you to stand up and take action. All the people in our life have the ability to inspire or to disempower us. We are influenced by every person we interact with, so if the goal is to create a new inspiring vision for our life, we must get intentional about who we surround ourselves with.

Unfortunately, this probably means there are people in your life right now who are not supporting your vision for a better life. There are probably people in your life who would prefer to see you stay right where you are rather than see you grow into an amazing human being. After all, when you change, they have a choice to make. They either have to change themselves or they have to move on. As long as they keep the focus on keeping you in line, then they don't have to work on themselves. So, keeping you right where you are becomes an unconscious endeavor for them.

If we want to tap into our power and create an inspiring story, we have to make conscious choices about who is in our circle. It may be unfortunate and hard, but it is also a necessity. Are the people in your circle inspiring you or sucking the life out of you? Are they supporting you or are they looking for ways to bring you "back to reality"? We have to ask these types of questions of all the people in our life, and then we have to make a choice. Who do we develop deeper relationships with, and who do we move away from?

It can be very challenging to accept that the people who've been in our life for decades are no longer supporting our new vision. They aren't bad people, but the fact is that they simply aren't helping you achieve your goals. Would we rather have the status quo or would we rather have growth?

It's worth noting that this process is not black and white. We aren't making a naughty and nice list. We don't have to completely write off everyone who doesn't wholeheartedly support our vision. You may choose to just spend less time with certain people. You may simply choose to become more aware when you are with certain people so you don't get sucked into their games.

Tailoring our relationships is less like a high school basketball coach cutting players and more about setting an intention about who we *do* want in our life. That act will naturally draw the people we want and repel those who are no longer serving our highest vision. Our inspiring inner circle will align perfectly with our intention.

The silver lining is that we also get to define and develop our inspiring relationships. These are the people we dig deeper with. We spend more time with them and have meaningful conversations that make everyone better. These are the relationships that need nurturing, and the act of nurturing those relationships is an investment into our vision. It is important to seek out people who love and support us along our journey. There is something magical about a group of friends who all support one another, when there is a close-knit group of people all working together toward a common goal.

This tailoring of friendships absolutely does not mean that everyone in our circle should be exactly the same. Diversity is inevitable and imperative to our growth. I have a very diverse group of friends, but my best friends are people whom I align with. I can count on them when I need them. I know I can go to them when I need support, and I know they will challenge me in a healthy way when I need it. We can talk openly and honestly, and we all learn from each other. Just being around these people inspires me. In their individual ways, each of them pushes me forward and makes me a better person.

We have limited energy and we have limited focus, so it's imperative that we become intentional. Our friends frequently direct our focus, so we must be selective with our circle as we continue our journey toward our highest vision. Although it hurts to drift from long-held friendships, creating space for new, more inspiring relationships makes this transition worthwhile.

INFLUENCERS

While tailoring our inner circle is imperative to living in our vision, taking stock of the influencers in our life is just as important. They may be close to us, they may be someone on TV, or they could be a coach. They may even be someone writing an awesome book, just like this one! Being intentional about whom you allow to influence your life and your choices just makes sense. Notice that I used the word *allow*. You have the ability to choose whom you allow to influence you. Just like so many things in life, you have a responsibility to become aware about your options and choices so you can make responsible decisions that ultimately lead you to your end goal.

Whether you have met them or not, as you take in their message, they have the power to shift your consciousness. Who has earned the privilege to have your attention? I challenge you to take this task extra seriously. This will have a large impact on your ability to grow into the person you and I both know you can be.

Once you become aware, you will begin to see how people and situations are influencing you. You will become aware of whether an influencer is inspiring your powerful vision or trying to take over your train. We tend to put a lot of faith and trust into our influencers, and rightfully so. These are the people we have tasked to help us grow and become better. Before you simply turn over the keys to someone else, make sure the person influencing your choices truly has your best interests in mind.

The work of personal growth is not a buzzword or a topic of conversation at a cocktail party; it's a lifestyle. Personal development has the power to completely change our life and, therefore, the world in an instant. With great power comes great responsibility, so take this journey seriously. It may be hard at first, but it gets easier … and then harder … and then easier again … and then harder again. But with every mistake, with every conversation, with every realization, you will find strength, power, and fortitude. Over time, these feelings of empowerment move you forward as you discover your inspiring story. And as you discover your inspiring story, taking the plunge into action will simply be a natural next step!

CHAPTER 11

TAKE THE PLUNGE

"Security is mostly a superstition ... Life is either
a daring adventure or nothing."

—Helen Keller

NOW IT'S TIME TO TAKE THE PLUNGE! Don't just stand there. Do something! All the ideas in this book are great, but unless we understand our past, discover our vision, move forward with intention, and immerse ourselves in the work, this is simply a bunch of words on a page. It's time to get out there and do the messy, fulfilling, and necessary work to change yourself and the world. Pursuing the vision you have created for yourself is energizing and fulfilling, and I am confident that once you catch the bug, there is no looking back. This is where the rubber hits the road. Are you up for the challenge to change the world with intention?

I recognize that it could be easy to get bogged down in the details from this book. It could be easy to think and think and think, all while actually doing nothing. It could be easy to criticize the content or to commiserate about your current circumstances. But while the easy road may feel safe and comfortable in the here and now, the reality is that the easy road ultimately leads to one of the most challenging existences out there: a life unfulfilled.

Like a train leaving the station, it takes a lot of energy to get the train moving, but once it's on its way, it moves with an effortless momentum that contains great power. Don't be a train that was destined to travel the countryside, yet sits in the station all because it was too hard to get started. Do the work to get your train moving and then tell the world to watch out. Stop playing it safe. Create action, get out of the station, and make the world better.

I'm a competitive guy, so I have found a strategy that leverages my competitiveness. I'm getting better, but the fact remains that I hate admitting I'm wrong. I also hate telling people that I fell short on a commitment. Because I know these things about myself, I often tell trusted people all about my ridiculous goals on the front end. Many times they look at me and say, "OK, good luck with that." Other times they fully support my idea. I don't put too much thought into their reactions, though. I simply tell them these thoughts and ideas, because I know I will hold myself accountable simply because I don't want to go back to those people and tell them I failed. This may or may not work for you, but it is just one of many strategies that may help you find some momentum.

Once you find a strategy that gets you moving in the right direction, you must then commit. Not to beat this train metaphor to death, but … if a train pumps the engines and starts to move forward, then cuts the engines a moment later, it once again becomes a useless lump of steel. It takes time and commitment for this giant object to get moving. The same is true for your soul. There are programs that are so engrained in your psyche that it takes time and energy to work through them. Give yourself the time to explore, and find the ways to give yourself the energy it takes to move your train out of the station. Keep moving forward. Keep looking for new ways to build momentum and commit to the process. It is hard to get your soul moving in a new direction. But once you experience the feeling of an unstoppable momentum behind you, you will never look back and no one will slow you down.

Once you make this commitment to yourself, please remember that you can't fail. You have already succeeded through the act of trying. If you have a vision and you put an intention behind that vision, then every experience is a success. Even when you experience setbacks, you will feel the success in your attempt. There are a few things that are important to keep in mind as you embark on your journey.

COMPASSION

As you begin to take the plunge into a new and more inspiring life, remember that as you grow and change, your world will change with you. All around you, people will look different, the world will become more vibrant and welcoming, relationships will form to fit your intentions and worldviews, and others will recognize the new and powerful person you have become. This new empowering worldview can be very exciting, but it can also stir the emotion pot. This means that as we embark on this journey, negative emotions may arise. Embrace these changes with compassion. Change always starts off with an unknown future, and when the future is unknown, fear and anxiety crash the party. That is OK and it's normal, so lean into the discomfort. The struggle is the indicator that great change and a new amazing life are coming forth. Since you know you are going to stretch yourself and bring discomfort, you must find compassion.

Part of showing compassion for yourself is the act of allowing yourself to *fully* feel what you feel. It is normal to feel uncertain, fearful, or anxious. So, rather than stuffing those feelings into the back of your train, embrace them and allow yourself to really experience them. If you feel fear, stop, close your eyes, look at your fear, lean into your fear, show love for your fear, and then continue to move forward. Be brave, and remember, bravery is not the lack of fear. Bravery is doing what you know is the right thing to do, even in the face of fear.

If you feel anger, yell at the top of your lungs, punch a pillow, name your anger, call that person all the names you want (not to their face, of course), and get it all out. Then take ten deep and long breaths and come back to your awareness. Recognize your anger and show your anger love. Then move forward and do what you truly believe is in alignment with your intention.

If you plan to experience your negative emotions fully, you must also commit to experiencing your positive emotions. On a recent call with my coach, I discovered that I had no intention of ever celebrating the completion of this book. I put all this time and energy into this process, and out of a shadow sense of humility, I was choosing to ignore my accomplishment. I was ready to move on to the next project without fully experiencing the joy and pride I felt. I now realize how this stifles my energy and makes it harder for me to continue along my journey. Whether your emotions are positive or negative, the key is to allow yourself to fully experience your emotions with compassion, and perhaps a bit of control, too.

I am definitely not suggesting that we blow up at the waiter who got our order wrong and then throw our food in his face as we storm out the door in an attempt to "express our frustration fully." It does, however, mean that we give ourselves permission to explore and feel our emotions at the right time and in the right place. Obviously, timing and self-control will be paramount for all this. But, be honest with yourself, experience your feelings fully, and acknowledge your true self. These are all forms of self-love and compassion and, thus, the path to wholeness.

BE HONEST AND FLEXIBLE

You may be able to fool your friends, your family, or even your significant other, but I promise that, deep down, you can never fool yourself. This process of personal development is built on the cornerstone of honesty. Give yourself permission to be brutally honest with yourself.

Your mind will play all sorts of tricks to keep you from discovering the truth, but if you stick with it, the truth will reveal itself. Through honesty, you will find deep-rooted secrets that you have hidden from yourself your entire life. You will find truths that hurt, but you will also find joy, liberation, and pride. Accept these truths and keep digging. The process can be frustrating sometimes. That is why flexibility becomes vitally important.

Your mind will tell you to stop. It will find all sorts of creative ways to derail your progress, so you must be willing to work with this and find new ways of thinking. This entire process is trial and error. Flexibility allows us to shift from one strategy to another as we search for the best option.

If you are truly honest with yourself and digging as deep as you can to discover your highest self, you will have to be flexible. Unlike the train (yep, back to that analogy), this work is not a straight path. It winds all over the place, and we have to be willing and able to "change the play" when needed.

Once again, this is where coaches come into play. They can challenge us when we aren't being wholly honest or when we attempt to hide. They can help us decipher the truths we are just beginning to understand. They can help us build strategies that we may be oblivious to. They can help us lighten up when we get discouraged. Ultimately, they keep us honest about the things we don't want to acknowledge, and they help us stay flexible as we change course.

Challenge yourself to look inward with complete honesty and without judgment, and then be flexible as you move forward.

MOURNING

Change is an odd thing sometimes. The dichotomy within the concept of change is that in order for something new to arise, something else must change or die. This can create a sense of mourning. In my experience, this sense of mourning has been less like the mourning of the death of a loved one, and more like a compassionate mourning that one might feel for a child who has just learned a valuable life lesson. We wish the child didn't have to go through the pain of changing and learning, but deep down, we know this is the path the child must take. Personal change can be very similar. In many ways, we are still like little children, just trying to find our place in this world as we figure it all out. As we learn and grow and discover new realizations, it is inevitable that part of us will die and our soul will grieve for the death. Even though our soul is fully aware that this death must take place, we will grieve. It is natural.

A few years back, I was in a time of great change in my life. My priorities were really shifting. I no longer wanted to gossip, argue over ceaseless political issues, tap into drama, and drink until two in the morning. I was realizing that I wanted to take care of my mind and body, and I knew I was changing. However, these practices were how I connected with my closest friends at the time. I was fearful that if I started telling them I didn't want to drink all night and get into dead-end conversations anymore, they would find me to be arrogant, lame, or maybe even holier than thou. I feared that they wouldn't understand my new worldview and my new priorities and, therefore, they would just stop hanging out with me.

I had to do a lot of self-reflection during this time, because I had to figure out whether my new priorities were really what I wanted. I had to figure out if this was all worth it. What good is having strong priorities and self-awareness if it alienates me from all my friends? Ultimately, I decided that I wanted to move my life forward. My friends would either accept it (although I didn't expect them to fully understand why I was changing), or they would move on and I would have fresh space for new people to enter my life.

This is a heavy realization. It brought up a lot of fear that transformed into mourning. A piece of me that had served me well for many years was now dying, and a new me was being born. This mourning lasted months. I felt sad that I couldn't explain to others why my life shifted. I felt sad that some of my relationships with close friends would never be the same. It was hard! But all my friends who I was so worried about losing have only become closer to me. The relationships are stronger than ever because I am living in my true self and they have accepted that. Additionally, some friendships that weren't serving my vision have fallen by the wayside, but as I suspected, this falling off opened the door for new, more productive relationships.

I needed to feel that fear. I needed to mourn. I'm glad I gave myself the time and space to feel my real emotions, because it gave me the opportunity to move on to a new chapter in my life with power and conviction.

There will be times as you grow when you will joyously celebrate, and there will be times when you will mourn the loss of a part of you that no longer serves your highest being.

Remember that although we are talking about mourning the death of a part of us, it's really more of a transformation. That piece that you have held so dear is not dying; it is just morphing, as a caterpillar transforms into a butterfly. The caterpillar didn't die, and it's not that the caterpillar was wrong, bad, ugly, or any other horrible thing. It was simply time for the caterpillar to transform into a butterfly. As human beings, we have the amazing power to do this over and over and over. This piece of you that "dies" is always there. It's always on your train, and it is always there to serve you when you need it.

Mourning is part of the process of transformation. Show gratitude for that piece that needs to move on, and thank that part of you for its service. Your gratitude and understanding of how this aspect has served you will be more than enough, and it will help the grieving process move forward. It can be hard to let go, but right now, it's time for a transformation and this is part of the natural cycle of life.

LIFELONG WORK

Acceptance is imperative. We must accept that this process has no beginning and no end. It is a never-ending journey that we choose to take on, because we know we can improve every single day. Sometimes I struggle with this idea, because it would be easier to know I am working toward some finite goal. However, this is not a finite task. This is an infinite journey.

The journey of personal growth is a process during which we are always trying, failing, learning, growing, building, pushing, and loving. Accepting that we are imperfect and that we always have room to grow will keep us engaged in the process. Within this work, we must accept that the journey is the jewel. The destination is a mirage. By simply trying, you have already accomplished your mission. Wake up tomorrow and work at it again. The journey itself will reward you handsomely.

A JOURNEY

The following story demonstrates the essence of our journey here on this earth. This is just an example, but it captures many aspects of our journey toward growth. It is meant to be a metaphor. Take from it what you will, but remember that at the end of the day, the more we recognize that we are simply playing a game and the more we lighten up and listen, the more we enjoy the ride.

Close your eyes, and let's pretend you are standing in a meadow in the middle of a vast rainforest. There are massive trees that seem to block out the sun. The ground is completely covered with lush, green moss, vines, bushes, and beautiful flowering plants. You stand in awe as you look at this forest and think about the amazing fact that this tiny little spot can sustain such a diverse and rich life force. As you stand there and consider entering, a blindfold is placed over your eyes and a taut section of rope is put into your hand. You are brand new to this type of experience, so you trust that your guide knows what they are doing. The intention of this exercise is for you to have an opportunity to experience the jungle with all your senses, except for your sight. Your ideas and expectations are fresh and full of hope. "This is going to be so much fun," you say to yourself.

As you stand there blindfolded, your other senses begin to light up. You take a few steps into the forest and you can feel the warm, damp air on your skin. All of a sudden, the forest seems to get really loud. *Where did all this noise come from?* you think. You can hear monkeys far off in the distance. You know monkeys can be dangerous, but they are far away and you trust your guide. Plus you have this rope, which, if you have faith, will lead you where you need to go. You also hear countless birds calling to one another. There is a constant buzzing of bugs as they fly all around you. The cacophony produced by the forest is nothing short of astonishing. This forest is clearly invigorated with life.

Suddenly you remember that you can't see anything, and you realize that losing your sight has opened up a whole new world. As you take a few more steps into the forest, your sense of smell fires up. The abundance of smells paints a picture of all the life in the forest. The mustiness from the moisture combines with the floral scent of plants and flowers to create a soothing aroma that seems to welcome and calm you. As you continue to stand there, you start to notice the temperature. A hint of sunlight touches your shoulders, and there is a cool breeze running past you as you really begin to sink into this moment. You feel totally at peace.

All of a sudden, without speaking, your guide touches your hand and gives you a gentle push forward along the rope. You know this is the last guidance you will receive from your guide. The rest of the journey will be led by your intuition and this one solitary rope. You follow the instruction from your leader and begin to move forward on your own. After about ten minutes of following the line, you begin to become aware of the fact that you have no idea where the rest of the group is, including your guide. Are you in the front, middle, or back? "Oh, well, it doesn't matter. Just enjoy yourself and experience the forest," you say to yourself.

After another thirty minutes of following the rope and experiencing the forest, you really begin to notice that you are all alone. You're pretty sure you simply have to follow the rope and it will lead you toward the final destination, but you really have no idea whether you are still on track or whether you are doing something wrong. *Was there another rope I was supposed to find?* Are you sure you are supposed to continue to walk? Maybe you are supposed to stop and meditate in order to take it all in. *Did I miss something from the instructor? Did I make a wrong turn? Maybe I should wait for the others.* You begin to feel a bit lost. Maybe you screwed this whole thing up. Maybe. Maybe not.

OK, deep breath. You know what you are supposed to do. Just follow the rope. It will take you where you want to go. All of a sudden, you hear the monkeys again. They are a bit closer this time, and a tinge of fear begins to set in. How far away are they? Are they mean? *Is there anyone around to protect me? What if the rope leads me right to them?* You are now beginning to question the faith you once had in this rope. Before, you could simply follow the rope and have faith that you would be safe, but now the monkeys are close, you don't know where your guide is, and you begin to question this entire exercise.

"I'm just going to stop for a minute and think about this," you say to yourself. You decide to just sit down and get quiet for a moment. You let go of the rope and as you sit on the ground, you feel the damp earth beneath you and the aroma of the forest becomes much more potent. For a moment, your mind reconnects with the beauty of the forest, and a slight calm comes over you as you feel the earth beneath you. OK, back to the task at hand. Time to think about what to do about these monkeys. Suddenly, a slight breeze blows across your face and you notice a beautiful smell. It smells like a flower you have never smelled before, but a beautiful fragrance nonetheless. You get on your hands and knees and crawl upwind, toward what you can only imagine is an amazing flower. As you continue your search, you eventually realize you are very close. You reach out with your hand and grab something that feels like a flower. You put it to your nose, and it smells so good. You sit for a while and enjoy this moment. You are at peace and you feel a connection to the forest. Suddenly you are snapped out of your peaceful trance as the monkeys call out again.

Oh no, I forgot about the monkeys, you think to yourself. In an instant, you know you need to do something to protect yourself. In a complete knee-jerk reaction, you stand up and start walking away from the monkey calls. Where you're going, you aren't totally sure, but you need to do something because … well, because you need to do something, anything, that's why. After all, something is better than nothing, right?

As you continue your random, unguided walk through the forest, you accidentally smack your shin on a fallen tree. "Ouch!" you yell. You rub your leg and keep walking. No time to stop and think, and no time to worry about pain. There are monkeys out there and you are alone. Just keep walking, try to avoid hurting yourself again, and more importantly, avoid those stupid monkeys.

After a while, the flower and the rope become distant memories. You have been on your own for so long now that you nearly forget all about your guide and the people in your group. You know they were there at one point, but no one is around and no one can help you now. They probably don't care anyway. You need to do this on your own. You're better off on your own anyway. You don't need them. If they did care, they would be here to fix this situation and ease your struggle. *But they aren't here, so I guess I am on my own.*

Your thoughts come back to your situation. There are monkeys, prickly bushes, and tree stumps out there just waiting to cause pain and inhibit you from getting to where you need to go. You begin to wonder what the point is in all this, and you wonder if maybe you should just stop. Then you won't bump your shin, fall down, or get scratched. In mid-thought, you remember the monkeys. They will find you. You can't just stop; you must push on. As you begin to walk again, you run questions through your mind. *Why am I here? Why did I do this to myself? I wonder what everyone else is doing? I wonder if I am doing better or worse than everyone else? Where do I need to go again? What do I need to do? How do I get out of this whole mess?* As you think, you walk. As you walk, you think. All the while, you are fully aware that the monkeys continue to get closer. Alone with your thoughts and with no one to help, you continue to run into things, stumble, trip, and cause yourself great pain.

After a while, feelings of fear, frustration, loneliness, worry, hopelessness, anxiety, and sadness begin to set in.

In a fit of frustration, you exclaim out loud, "This isn't working anymore!" Everything you do just brings more problems. There is no clear path. You don't know where you came from, and you don't know where you are going or how to get there. As you think about your situation and everything that is going wrong, tears begin to stream down your face. This is so hopeless. You are lost, scared, and feeling completely helpless.

Once again you sit down and begin to think to yourself, *This is so hopeless. Everything I do is wrong. I'll never figure this out. I GIVE UP!* As you lean into your true expression of your feelings of frustration and fear, you are able to suddenly notice a sense of calm rush over your body. It's almost like you pushed all the negative emotions right out of your body. As if the act of aligning with what you truly feel and allowing yourself to express those feelings fully have allowed you to open up a conduit for clarity.

In this moment of exhaustion, you take a moment and just stop thinking. You simply sit there and get quiet. Suddenly, as if there was something directly guiding you, it dawns on you. *There was a rope! I remember that my original intention was to simply follow the rope as I enjoyed my journey through the forest. It's so simple! How did I ever get so lost!? The rope will guide me to where I need to go.*

OK, so how do I find the rope? you ask yourself. Maybe you can walk in one direction and hope you set out in the right one. Maybe you can yell for help in hopes of finding another person to lead you to the rope. Maybe you should just give up. Maybe you can walk in a circle that stretches bigger and bigger over time, until you find the rope.

Your conscious mind is coming up with all sorts of creative ideas, but none of them seems to be the right answer. As the correct answer continues to elude you, frustration and panic set in once again.

Then a new idea pops into your head. Remember what happened the last time you simply sat and got quiet? The quiet space seemed to bring some clarity. So, you sit down and get quiet.

Your mind begins to become still, and you find yourself asking for guidance. You don't know who or what you are asking guidance from, but after you ask for direction, you sit and listen. Suddenly, as if there was something directly telling you, an answer floats into your consciousness. This would be so much easier if you could see. Oh wow, you have been blind this whole time. Why hadn't you thought about this before? The answer has been right in front of your eyes this whole time, literally. Just take this stupid blindfold off, and this will be so much easier.

You take off the blindfold, and a whole new world opens up again. It's not that it had actually disappeared; it's just that you stopped seeing it as you once had. But now, you can see again! You see the color and the life. It is truly amazing. After a moment of taking it all in, you begin to feel hopeful, happy, and motivated to move forward. This new realization is invigorating. Fear, if only for a moment, is a thing of the past. You know what you need to do, and there is no turning back now! All you need to do is find the rope. Rejuvenated, you begin your search. You are driven forward by this knowing within yourself that the rope will appear if you just keep looking.

You take a few steps and then you see it. Only a few feet away from where you were sitting is the rope. Just like the forest, the rope never vanished and you never really strolled that far away. It just felt like you did.

At this moment, faith, trust, and determination begin to fill your soul as you grab onto the rope and embark on your journey. You now understand that the rope has always been there, ready to lead you to your destination. All you needed was trust. Trust that the universe is here to support you. Trust that you already have all the answers you need within you. Trust that you can find the answers. Trust that you are powerful.

As you walk, holding onto the rope, a new perspective begins to build and it all starts to make sense. You always knew the goal, but at some point you allowed the outside world to distract you from your true calling. As you drifted further and further away, fear, panic, and frustration set in. Once you were able to recognize the panic, you found an awareness of the world around you and you gained the power of choice. Then as you sat and got quiet and leaned into the struggle, the answers came. Out of this stillness, you found a new perspective and a new fortitude to move forward with intention and confidence. It's almost too simple, but you realize that when you quiet your mind and have faith that a lifeline is always there to guide you (whether you see it or not), you will have what you want and need in life. Through your struggles, you were given a gift. This gift comes in the form of experience. You can now draw off of this experience and tap into this knowledge anytime you want.

As you come to this realization, you smile to yourself. You continue to follow the rope, and as you travel, you notice an abundance of details in the forest. Every few steps you stop to admire a new plant, a new flower, a new bug. You still hear the monkeys, but it's weird: They don't seem generate anxiety in you anymore. They are still exactly the same, but through this new lens, you see them as being part of this forest, rather than a menace you need to fear. Their call is now a beautiful part of this whole experience rather than a point of stress. You begin to feel like you, yourself, are a part of the forest. You feel at peace. You are at one with yourself and with your world.

Eventually, the rope leads to a meadow. Some of your friends are there, and some of them are not. Some of them were very intentional about following the rope and doing exactly what they were told. Those friends saw some success, but just like you, there were struggles with their journey. They still had their blindfolds on and were wondering what was happening around them. It hadn't even crossed their minds to take off the blindfold. To your right, there are a few people who have giant smiles on their faces. They know they won the race and were the first ones to get to the meadow. They have a hard time telling you what they experienced. Their fixation on the finish line completely overshadowed the experience of the journey. Others still remain in the forest. They may be lost, they may be distracted, they may be scared, or they may be calm. For a moment you consider going back into the forest to help them, but a calmness overcomes you and a voice reminds you that they need to take their own journey. They need the struggle and the triumph. It is their journey. Don't take that away from them.

As you look around at everyone, you realize no one journey is better or worse than the other. They are just different. Everyone experienced some form of success and some form of failure. It's a give and take. As you imagine each person's journey, a wave of love rolls over you as you begin to truly understand we are all connected. We are all part of the same life force. Our lives may look completely different, but the fact is that we are much more alike than you ever thought possible. Every person in this meadow had the same goal in mind, and although all the journeys were unique, in the end, our objectives are very similar. We all just want to find our meadow.

You decide to sit again and quiet your mind one more time. As you think back on your own journey, you realize that every time you trusted guidance and let the energy of the universe, God, or the Superconscious flow through you, everything was so much easier. Worry, pain, frustration, strife, and anxiety melted away and you were free to think clearly again. You were able to focus on solutions rather than fear and problems.

TRUST

This is how the energy force works. The more we struggle against the force of nature, the more we struggle in all facets of life. When we let fear grip us and when we let ourselves get distracted, we begin to lose our ability to think clearly. When we choose to be present with our circumstances and recognize that we don't have all the answers, a whole new world opens up and we begin to realize that we have been wearing a blindfold our entire life. By looking at our life with honesty, we can find our blindfolds and remove them. When we ignore ourselves and play the game called "everything is fine," we are destined to walk in the forest blindfolded and alone.

When we simply shut off our brains from time to time and trust our gut, answers will flow. There is a guiding force in all our lives. It has always been there, and it will always be there. The universe is here to guide you if you just take the time to listen. It is always there, just like the rope. But when we decide to do it on our own, we end up walking all over an unknown forest with no direction. When we realize the rope is always there and have faith that it always leads us to our true calling, we have the freedom to enjoy every moment as we travel toward the best version of ourselves.

This feeling of being one with the world may seem a little "pie in the sky," or it may even seem careless. We can't all just walk around like we have no care in the world. We have to work. We have to support our family. So how can we possibly become one with the world, chill out, and still get out there and make things happen? That is a valid question. The irony is that the act of asking that question is both the reason we stay trapped in our old ways and the key to moving forward.

All I can say is that I have tapped into this power many times, and my life is better off for it. I put less energy into frustration and anger, and I put more energy into thinking about, planning, and creating the life that I want ... with clarity. That means I create more with less. If you have no idea what I am talking about, try getting quiet. Once you experience this feeling of powerful change deep within yourself, there is no turning back. Once you learn to tap into your own personal power, the world opens up and you can only move forward toward a better life and toward what you truly want.

The bottom line is that, if we want to change the world with intention, we must first accept that we are completely full of it, and then work to change our internal world. To create change within ourselves, we have to discover who we are, where we want to go, and how we intend to get there.

We must be willing to try, fail, and try again. Then we can learn and grow all while recognizing that we actually have no real understanding about why we are here on this earth. Let's take the plunge, play the game, and enjoy the ride.

ENJOY THE RIDE

Let's discuss it one more time! Play with your experience. This is your one shot at life, so make it count by enjoying the ride. The world is your sandbox. Build it, shake it up, invite your friends, make a mess, pick up the pieces, do it again. It is so easy to get caught up in all the details of life. We are programmed to worry and despair, and although there are gifts in these traits, don't take life or yourself too seriously. Worrying, complaining, dramatics, hatred, and anger may feel good when we are challenged, but in the end, they are nothing more than distractions. If you are going to distract yourself, why not distract yourself with a playful curiosity about life? At the very least, you will probably enjoy the ride much more.

Lightening up begins with the acceptance that we are all full of it. Every … single … one of us. Even the greatest people out there have no idea what this life is all about. They might think they know what they are doing, but at the end of the day, this life is a vain attempt to figure it all out. I don't know that we will ever really know what life is all about, but I do know that the more we work together, the closer we will get to the answer, and the more fun we will have while we work to figure it out.

Our life is essentially a series of events. These events replay over and over, and as we grow, we learn and we interact with our world in different ways. Sometimes our lessons build us up and sometimes they tear us down, but as we become more aware, we gain the power of choice. As we gain the power of choice, we gain the power of freedom. As we gain the power of freedom, we are given the benefit of focused intention. As we gain the benefit of focused intention, we gain the gifts of happiness, fulfillment, and contentment.

OUR TEAM

Once we begin to realize our hidden potential, our power is uncontainable. As powerful as we are as individuals, think of the extraordinary power we wield as a team.

I purposely use the terms "we" and "us" a lot in this book, because this is *our* journey. We are on this planet together, and we are all learning and growing together. Our life experiences bind us together. Ultimately, that is why I wrote this book—to point out how similar we are, to challenge us to look inward, to help us learn how we can do things better, and to help us discover how we powerful we really are.

While I don't claim to have all the answers, I do claim to have some ideas, and I am doing what I can to raise the energy of the world. I have a desire to be part of the solution and bring others toward the discovery of their own untapped power.

I am asking that you join me in a lifelong journey to become the very best that we can be. Join me as we discover who we really are. Join me as we discover our power. Join me in being the change that we want to see in the world. Join me as we look to make the world a better place for ourselves and for generations to come.

As I write this book and as I share my stories, I am experiencing all the same struggles and emotions that we all feel. I am taking a risk, and I am trying to lead by example. I am excited for the opportunity to play in the sandbox every day. I may speak like I have all the answers, but I am not perfect and my work will continue for the rest of my life, which is exactly as it should be.

Just like you, I have come a long way in my journey, and I have a long way to go. But by trying, I am so much happier, so much calmer, and ultimately so much more content. Playing the game every day can be a challenge, but for me, I can now play the game with a sense of awareness and joy as I strive to change the world in my own unique way.

I have mentioned the word "challenge" many times in this book, because, in the end, this book is a challenge. It is a challenge to do something different and a challenge for you to risk standing out. My intention with this book is to challenge your perceptions about what you think you know about who you are and where you see your place in this world. I am challenging you to consider how powerful you are, and I am challenging you to take that knowledge and do something with it. It's easy to say, "I am powerful" as you sit on the couch and watch TV. It's another thing altogether to get off the couch and kick some ass. This is your life, your time, and your world. What are you going to do to change the world with intention today?

I am excited for you and for your journey. Yes, we are completely full of it, and I wouldn't have it any other way. Here is to your journey, here is to my journey, and here is to changing the world together!

APPENDICES

APPENDIX: CHART OF ROADBLOCKS

ROADBLOCK THAT CREATES STRUGGLE	BENEFITS OF AVOIDING THE STRUGGLE (why we choose to continue the struggle)	DRAWBACKS OF AVOIDING THE STRUGGLE	GIFT FROM ACCEPTANCE OF AND MOVING THROUGH STRUGGLE
Lack of self-reflection	Ignorance is bliss, denial is a hell of a drug, easy and comfortable	Disillusionment, untapped potential, pessimism, ignorance, stagnation	Awareness, choice, steadfastness, understanding of who you are and where you came from, fortitude, world changer
Lack of awareness	No need to address past pain and suffering, can keep on with the status quo, easy and comfortable	Missed growth opportunities, ignorance, destined to repeat life struggles, stagnation	Awareness of your stories and autopilot programs, power to change with intention and confidence, world changer
Blame	No personal responsibility, fun to talk about people's problems, you're never wrong, ego feels good, easy and comfortable	No positive change, anger, frustration, turmoil, loneliness, hatred, distraction, aimlessness, pessimism, stagnation	Intentional life, connectedness, ability to learn and grow, serenity, pride, integrity, world changer
Lack of purpose	Don't have to worry about failure, no risk with no plan, can fall back into routine and predictability, easy and comfortable	Aimlessness, boredom, self-loathing, pessimism, unfulfillment, stagnation	Intentional existence, vision, fulfillment, energy, clarity, confidence, zest for life, excitement, world changer
Lack of alignment	No accountability, don't have to create a plan, easy and comfortable	Distraction, lack of motivation, apathy, indecisiveness, lethargy, stagnation	Clarity of purpose, a knowing, confidence, creativity, vision, power, world changer
Lack of integrity	Ego is happy, you can focus on yourself, easy and comfortable	Self-loathing, blaming, loneliness, apathy, indecisiveness, aimlessness, stagnation	Self-confidence, soundness of sleep, trustworthiness, strength, pride, world changer

Distractions	Much more fun than seeing a therapist, in the know about "the haps" on TV and news, easy and comfortable	No time for reflection, unconscious, scattered, lacking confidence, tired, angry, ignorant, neglectful, blaming, stagnant	Focus, creation, vision, alignment, fortitude, world changer
Lack of physical awareness	Don't have to eat healthy, don't have to get a gym membership, easy and comfortable	Poor health, exhaustion, uncertainty, lack of motivation, depression, stagnation	Healthy lifestyle, healthy mindset, longevity, energy, awareness, vitality, confidence, world changer
Poor eating habits	No cauliflower, McDonald's is delicious, ice cream, easy and comfortable	Lethargy, lack of motivation, tiredness, poor health, shortened life, stagnation	Energy, longevity, healthy appearance, pride, ability to turn heads, confidence, world changer
Lack of physical activity	Stay in comfort zone, can binge watch any show you want, easy and comfortable	Poor health, shortened life, pain, unfulfillment, regret, exhaustion, depression, stagnation	Motivation, energy, confidence, strength, dedication, vitality, sense of accomplishment, pride, world changer
Lack of attention to physical appearance	Don't have to buy new clothes, only have to do hair/brush teeth on work days, easy and comfortable	Self-doubt, timidity, uncertainty, stagnation	Confidence, presence, pride, power, world changer
Lack of sleep	Get to binge watch Netflix, more time to work or exercise, don't have to put yourself to bed early	Lethargy, fogginess, loss of motivation, emotional swings, depression, tiredness, lack of awareness	More energy, focus, awareness, vision, motivation, happiness, rested, clarity, vitality, world changer
Fear	No reason to risk, excuses are easy and comfortable	Scared, tired, sad, unfulfilled, scattered, unconscious, unintentional, worried, stagnant	Bravery, self-discovery, power, confidence, strength, knowledge, wholeness, world changer
Trying to do it on your own	Bragging rights if successful, no one will know if you fail, don't have to rely on others	Unsuccessful, confused, scattered, frustrated, worried, powerless, stagnant	Connectedness, purpose, self-realization, validation, clarity, confidence, world changer

APPENDIX: GUIDED MEDITATION
FOR INTENTION-SETTING

As we move into setting new intentions, I think it makes sense to do a quick guided meditation. If you are listening, find a quiet place and follow along. If you are reading this, then read through the meditation and do your best to follow the practice.

Find a comfortable place to sit or lie down. Close your eyes. Take a moment and allow an intention to come into your conscious mind. If nothing comes to mind, that is perfectly fine. If something does come to your mind, think about that intention, internalize it, and then let it go. It's still within you, but let it slip out of your conscious mind. Bring your attention to your third eye (just above your eyes in the center of your forehead). Sit quietly and as you take the next five breaths, bring your attention to your breathing. Stay here for as long as you like. Feel your chest fill with aireand then empty. Feel the air flow through your nose and mouth. Stay here for as long as you like, and just relax into your breath. If you ever find your mind drifting, simply come back to your breath.

Now take a moment to check in with your body. Do a body scan to see if you are holding tension anywhere. Check in with your face and relax all the muscles. Relax your eyes, relax your cheeks, and relax your mouth. Come back to your breath and feel your breath go in and out a few times. Next, move to your neck. Do you have any tension? If so, relax your neck and let it go. Come back to your breath and feel your breath go in and out a few times. Next move to your shoulders. Do you have any tension? If so, relax your shoulders and let it go. Come back to your breath. Feel your breath go in and out a few times. Now move to your chest and stomach. Do you have any tension? If so, relax your chest and stomach and let it go. Come back to your breath again and feel your breath go in and out a few times. Now move to your legs. Do you have any tension? Relax your legs and let it go.

Now that your body is relaxed, simply sit with yourself and the universe. Your conscious mind is not needed. There is still an appreciation for your conscious mind, but it's not needed here. Focus on your breath and simply be. Stay here for as long as you like, and open yourself up to receiving something from the universe. You don't need to think. Just sit and listen.

When you are ready, take a moment to thank yourself and to thank the universe. You have done great work here today. As you bring your awareness back to your body, wiggle your fingers and toes and become aware of the room around you. Feel the air, and bring your attention back to any sensations you feel. When you are ready, open your eyes. Take one more giant breath in and let it out with a very audible sigh.

ACKNOWLEDGMENTS

THIS BOOK MAY HAVE my name on the cover, but I must give credit for the completion of these pages to all the amazing people in my life. Without the support of so many, this book would not be in existence. I am truly grateful for all of you who have touched my life over the past 40 years.

Thank you to my wife, Allison. I have no idea how many hours we have spent over the past 15 years analyzing, talking, and debating all life has to offer. What I do know is how I have learned from your wisdom. We may never have it all figured out, but I am so thankful to have a partner who always has my back and who is always there when I need you. You are an amazing human, and I am blessed to have you as my partner, confidant, wife, and friend.

Thank you to my kids, Caleb and Kailia. There are some things in life you can learn only through the experience of being a father, and I am so thankful you are in my life. Your influence has reminded me to keep trying, slow down, enjoy life, smile more, and remember the small things. Many of the substantial changes I have made in my life were either for you or as a direct result of the little truth bombs you are so good at delivering. I am so proud of you both!

Thank you to my parents. We may have disagreed at times (maybe), but you always had my best interests in mind. For that, I am eternally grateful. Without your support and love for me, I might not be here today and I surely would not be the man I am. Thank you for your honesty and love.

Thank you to my brothers and my sister for sharing all your hard truths and for setting an amazing example. I am so grateful for our time together and for your support.

Thank you to all my coaches and teachers. Susan Tzankow, you walked with me through some of my toughest days as I worked to understand my own shadows. Your support has been crucial to my healing. Rick Harrigan, your positive energy and amazing wisdom have served me long before and long after we actually worked together. And Courtland Warren, I am so grateful for you and your sage advice. Through your dedication to the growth and success of others, you make the world a better place, every day. Your honest feedback and support of my journey have been instrumental to my growth and the completion of this book.

Thank you to my friends. I am truly blessed to be surrounded by so many great people who entertain, challenge, and brighten my life. If who we are today is the culmination of the influences of our few closest friends, then I am proud of who I have become. Thank you for your support, and thank you for being awesome!

ABOUT THE AUTHOR

DAN GOMER is a teacher turned entre-
preneur. After leaving the classroom, Dan
turned his sights to real estate as an investor, broker, and team leader. Leveraging
these experiences, Dan has come full
circle as he looks to once again teach
and inspire others through writ-ing and speaking. Dan lives in
Highlands Ranch, Colorado, with his wife and two kids.